A Beginner's Guide to SSD Firmware

Designing, Optimizing, and Maintaining SSD Firmware

Gopi Kuppan Thirumalai

Apress®

A Beginner's Guide to SSD Firmware: Designing, Optimizing, and Maintaining SSD Firmware

Gopi Kuppan Thirumalai
San Jose, CA, USA

ISBN-13 (pbk): 978-1-4842-9887-9   ISBN-13 (electronic): 978-1-4842-9888-6
https://doi.org/10.1007/978-1-4842-9888-6

Managing Director, Apress Media LLC: Welmoed Spahr
Acquisitions Editor: Smriti Srivastava
Development Editor: Laura Berendson
Editorial Assistant: Jessica Vakili
Copy Editor: April Rondeau

Cover designed by eStudioCalamar

Cover image by Michael Dziedzic on Unsplash (www.unsplash.com)

Distributed to the book trade worldwide by Springer Science+Business Media New York, 1 New York Plaza, Suite 4600, New York, NY 10004-1562, USA. Phone 1-800-SPRINGER, fax (201) 348-4505, email orders-ny@springer-sbm.com, or visit www.springeronline.com. Apress Media, LLC is a California LLC and the sole member (owner) is Springer Science + Business Media Finance Inc (SSBM Finance Inc). SSBM Finance Inc is a **Delaware** corporation.

For information on translations, please e-mail booktranslations@springernature.com; for reprint, paperback, or audio rights, please e-mail bookpermissions@springernature.com.

Apress titles may be purchased in bulk for academic, corporate, or promotional use. eBook versions and licenses are also available for most titles. For more information, reference our Print and eBook Bulk Sales web page at http://www.apress.com/bulk-sales.

Any source code or other supplementary material referenced by the author in this book is available to readers on GitHub (github.com/apress). For more detailed information, please visit https://www.apress.com/gp/services/source-code.

Paper in this product is recyclable

To my mother, Vijaya T, and my father,
Thirumalai J

Table of Contents

TABLE OF CONTENTS

About the Author

Gopi Kuppan Thirumalai is a highly experienced embedded design engineer with a proven track record of success in the industry. He has over 15 years of experience in a variety of domains, including wireless networks, software, automotive, and storage. He is an expert in client and data-center SSD design and implementation and has a history of leading and mentoring teams to achieve their goals. He is also an outdoor enthusiast and enjoys hiking, fitness, reading books, and cooking.

About the Technical Reviewer

Kenneth Fukizi is a software engineer, architect, and consultant with experience internationally in coding on different platforms. Prior to dedicated software development, he worked as a lecturer and was then head of IT at different organizations. He has domain experience working with technology for companies mainly in the financial sector. When he's not working, he likes reading up on emerging technologies and strives to be an active member of the software community.

Kenneth currently leads a community of African developers through a startup company called AfrikanCoder.

CHAPTER 1

Introduction to SSD Firmware

Welcome to the world of SSD firmware! This chapter marks the beginning of your journey into the intricate world of solid-state drive (SSD) firmware. In this chapter, I will lay the foundation by exploring the fundamental concepts and essential aspects of SSD firmware. My goal is to provide you with a clear understanding of what SSDs are, the role of firmware in optimizing their performance, and the key differences that set SSDs apart from traditional hard-disk drives (HDDs).

What Is SSD?

A solid-state drive (SSD) is a type of storage device that uses flash memory to store data. Compared to traditional hard drives, which use spinning disks to store data, SSDs are much faster, more reliable, and more energy efficient. However, to take full advantage of the capabilities of an SSD, it is necessary to use specialized software known as SSD firmware. SSD firmware is the embedded software that controls the functions and features of an SSD. It is responsible for managing the storage, retrieval, and protection of data on the drive. SSD firmware is typically stored on the drive's non-volatile memory and is executed by the drive's controller when the drive is powered on. It plays a critical role in ensuring the reliable and efficient operation of an SSD.

© Gopi Kuppan Thirumalai 2023
G. Kuppan Thirumalai, *A Beginner's Guide to SSD Firmware*,
https://doi.org/10.1007/978-1-4842-9888-6_1

The first SSD, introduced in the late 1970s, used simple firmware that was primarily responsible for interfacing with the host system and translating its commands into actions on the drive. At the beginning, SSDs were introduced for use in early IBM supercomputers, but they were not often used due to their high cost. Over time, as SSD technology has evolved, the firmware has become increasingly complex, adding features such as wear leveling, garbage collection, and encryption. In addition, the capabilities of SSD firmware have improved over time to support larger SSDs, with current firmware able to support drives with capacities of up to 100 TB or more.

Today, SSD firmware is a crucial component of modern storage systems, providing numerous benefits over traditional hard disk drives (HDDs), such as faster access to data, higher reliability, and lower power consumption. It also enables advanced features such as data protection, power management, and error correction, which are essential for maintaining the integrity and performance of the drive.

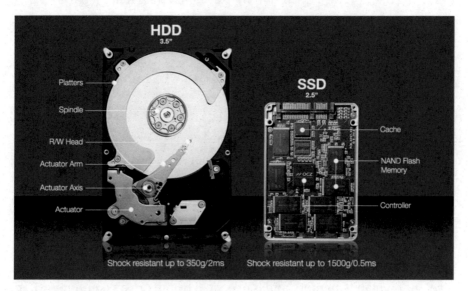

Figure 1-1. *Comparison of HDD and SSD*

In addition to supporting larger SSDs, modern SSD firmware is also designed to improve the performance of the drive. For example, SSD firmware can optimize the process of reading and writing data to the drive, and it can also improve the reliability of the drive by using techniques such as error-correcting code (ECC) and wear leveling.

There are several different types of SSD that are commonly used, including data-center SSDs, client SSDs, external SSDs, and enterprise SSDs. Each of these types of SSD has its own unique set of requirements, and the firmware that is used with these drives is specifically designed to meet those requirements.

One important consideration when designing SSD firmware is the type of memory that is used in the drive. The most common types of memory used in SSDs are single-level cell (SLC), multi-level cell (MLC), triple-level cell (TLC), and quadruple-level cell (QLC). Each of these types of memory has its own unique characteristics, and the firmware that is used with the drive must be optimized to take advantage of those characteristics. SLC memory is generally considered to be the most reliable and robust type of memory, but it is also the most expensive. MLC, TLC, and QLC memory are generally less expensive than other types, but they are also less reliable and have lower endurance, meaning they can't withstand as much wear and tear (less P/E cycle (program/erase Cycle) compared to SLC). In addition, the firmware design and implementation for MLC, TLC, and QLC memory can be more complex compared to other types of memory. This means that the firmware used to control and manage the memory may be more intricate and require more effort to design and implement. In general, MLC, TLC, and QLC memory are less durable and more complex to work with compared to other types of memory, but they can be a cost-effective option for certain applications.

Another important consideration when designing SSD firmware is the type of host interface that is supported. The host interface is the interface that connects the SSD to the rest of the system, and different interfaces have different performance characteristics. The most common types of host interface for SSDs are SATA, USB, NVMe, and SAS (Serial-Attached Small Computer System Interface (SCSI). SATA is the most common and widely supported interface, but it has relatively low performance compared to other interfaces. NVMe is a newer interface that is designed specifically for high-performance storage devices, and it can provide much higher performance than SATA. USB is a universal interface that is commonly used for external storage devices, but it has lower performance than other interfaces. SAS is a high-performance interface that is commonly used in enterprise storage systems, but it is not as widely supported as SATA or NVMe.

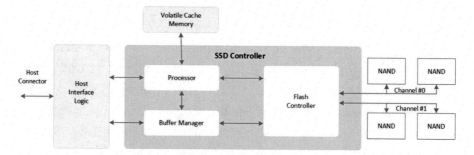

Figure 1-2. SSD block diagram

This book is a basic resource that covers the fundamental principles and technical aspects of SSD firmware and is designed to provide a basic understanding of the key concepts and technologies used in SSD firmware. The guide is divided into several chapters, each of which covers a different aspect of SSD firmware. The first few chapters provide an overview of SSD firmware, including the key features and benefits of SSDs and the ways in which they differ from traditional hard-disk drives (HDDs). These chapters help with understanding the role of the SSD firmware in managing the read and write operations of the drive and also dive into the history and evolution of SSD firmware.

The further chapters delve into the inner workings of SSD firmware, exploring fundamental NAND operations, various techniques for error correction, and strategies for endurance management. They also cover common SSD firmware features, design considerations, and the all-important flash translation layer. The chapters then examine the flow of user data and exception handling in an SSD, as well as performance optimization and debugging support. Finally, the book concludes with a look to the future, examining the cutting-edge technologies and innovations that are shaping the future of SSD firmware.

This book may provide a valuable resource for anyone interested in understanding the technical details of SSD firmware basics and how firmware impacts the performance and reliability of solid-state drives. Whether you are a firmware engineer, a computer science student, or simply someone interested in learning more about SSDs, this book is sure to provide you with a basic information and insights.

Summary

In this chapter, we covered the basics of SSD firmware. You have learned that SSD firmware is the software that controls the operation of an SSD. You have also learned that SSD firmware is responsible for tasks such as managing the wear leveling of the NAND flash memory, garbage collection, and error correction.

You have also learned about the different types of SSD that are commonly used, including data center SSDs, client SSDs, external SSDs, and enterprise SSDs. We have discussed the different types of memory that are used in SSDs, such as SLC, MLC, TLC, and QLC. We have also looked at the different types of host interfaces that are supported by SSDs, such as SATA, USB, NVMe, and SAS. This chapter set the stage for a deeper dive into the intricate workings of SSD firmware, promising insights into NAND operations, error correction techniques, performance optimization, and future innovations.

CHAPTER 2

Understanding the Role of Firmware in SSDs

Picture the hardware of a solid-state drive (SSD) as the engine of a car, and the firmware as the driver who controls and optimizes its performance. In the SSD world, firmware takes center stage, fine-tuning every interaction between the physical components and the digital world. This chapter embarks on a journey to unveil the firmware's pivotal role in SSDs, breaking down its intricate responsibilities and how it makes things happen.

What Is Firmware?

For SSDs to work properly and help us with tasks, they rely on both hardware and firmware. The hardware consists of the physical components of the device, such as the processor, memory, and storage. The firmware, meanwhile, is the software that runs on the device and controls the hardware. It is responsible for ensuring that the device performs its designated tasks and functions properly.

© Gopi Kuppan Thirumalai 2023
G. Kuppan Thirumalai, *A Beginner's Guide to SSD Firmware*,
https://doi.org/10.1007/978-1-4842-9888-6_2

The primary role of SSD firmware is to manage the storage, retrieval, and protection of data on the drive. Firmware is typically embedded into the hardware during the manufacturing process and is not intended to be modified by the user.

In SSDs, firmware plays a crucial role in the performance and functionality of the drive. It controls the various hardware components of the drive, such as the memory chips and interface controller, and manages the data stored on the SSD. Additionally, SSD firmware provides many advanced features that are essential for maintaining the performance and reliability of the drive. For example, it can include wear-leveling algorithms that distribute data evenly across the drive to prevent excessive wear on any one area of the drive, garbage-collection algorithms that reclaim unused space on the drive to improve performance, and algorithms to reduce write amplification. (Write amplification is a process that increases the amount of data written to the drive beyond the amount of data that the user writes.)

SSD firmware can also include encryption capabilities to protect data on the drive, as well as power-management functions to help conserve energy and extend the lifespan of the drive. These features are essential for modern SSDs, which are often used in high-performance computing environments and require the highest levels of data protection and reliability.

Additionally, SSD firmware is responsible for managing the internal data structures of the drive, such as the journaling data that is used to keep track of changes to the data on the drive. This allows the drive to recover from any errors or power failures that may occur.

Another important function of SSD firmware is to manage thermal throttling, which is the process by which the drive reduces its performance in order to prevent overheating. This can help to protect the drive from damage and extend its lifespan.

When we use our devices, they often run multiple programs at the same time. Over time, this can lead to a decrease in system performance and slower operation. One solution to this problem is to replace the hardware with new parts. However, this can be expensive and time-consuming. A more cost-effective and simpler solution is to update the firmware that the system runs on. Firmware updates can fix bugs, improve performance, and add new features to the device, all without the need to replace any hardware.

Firmware updates for SSDs can be installed by the user and are typically available for download from the manufacturer's website. It is important to keep the firmware of an SSD up to date to get the most out of the drive and to ensure its proper functioning.

Updating the firmware on an SSD can bring several benefits, including improved performance, increased stability, and access to new features. For example, a firmware update may optimize the performance of the drive by improving instruction times, out-of-order execution, branch prediction, and speculative execution time. It may also fix bugs that have developed over time and prevent the need for expensive repairs or bug fixes in the future.

In addition to these benefits, updating the firmware on an SSD can help to prevent the drive from becoming obsolete. By adopting the additional functionalities and capabilities that come with the firmware update, users can ensure that their SSD remains compatible with newer technologies and is able to keep up with changing needs.

Finally, SSD firmware is responsible for managing the mapping of logical block addresses to physical block addresses on the drive. This is necessary because the data on the drive is typically organized into blocks, and the firmware must manage the mapping of these blocks to the actual physical locations on the drive where the data is stored. This is an essential part of the drive's overall performance and reliability.

Summary

This chapter pulled back the curtain on the unsung hero of SSDs: firmware. Think of it as the conductor of an orchestra, ensuring each instrument (component) plays in harmony to create a beautiful symphony (performance). Firmware's primary job is to manage data storage, retrieval, and safeguarding. It makes sure no single spot on the drive wears out prematurely and reclaims space that's not being used. It even handles tricky maneuvers like reducing the amount of data written, thus extending the drive's lifespan. Firmware is also the brain behind encryption and energy-saving tricks, crucial in today's demanding computing world.

The chapter also highlighted firmware updates, like giving your car a software upgrade. These updates fine-tune the drive's performance, fix bugs, and even add new features without needing to swap parts. They're your SSD's way of staying sharp and relevant, much like updating your phone's software. Lastly, firmware's task of mapping logical data to physical locations was emphasized—the GPS of your SSD, ensuring data arrives at its destination smoothly. This chapter has shown that firmware is the true wizard behind the scenes of SSD engineering.

CHAPTER 3

The History and Evolution of SSD Firmware

In this chapter, we delve into the historical evolution of solid-state drive (SSD) firmware, tracing its journey from its rudimentary origins to its present-day complexities. Our exploration begins with the early days of SSD technology, when firmware was a modest tool focused on basic interfacing tasks. As time progressed, firmware transitioned into a powerhouse of advanced functionalities. Our analysis concludes by examining the contemporary challenges and innovative solutions that underscore the realm of SSD firmware engineering.

History

The history of SSD firmware can be traced back to the early days of SSD technology, when the first SSDs were introduced in the late 1970s. At that time, SSD firmware was a relatively simple piece of software that was primarily responsible for interfacing with the host system and translating its commands into actions on the drive.

© Gopi Kuppan Thirumalai 2023
G. Kuppan Thirumalai, *A Beginner's Guide to SSD Firmware*,
https://doi.org/10.1007/978-1-4842-9888-6_3

Early SSD firmware was focused on ensuring data integrity and reliability. This was important because early SSDs were prone to data loss due to the instability of its memory. To address this issue, early SSD firmware included basic features such as error-correction algorithms. These algorithms were used to detect and correct errors in the data stored on the drive, improving the reliability and integrity of the data.

Over the next several decades, as SSD technology continued to evolve, the firmware also evolved to include more advanced features and capabilities. For example, early SSDs lacked the wear-leveling algorithms that are now commonly found in modern drives, which distribute data evenly across the drive to prevent excessive wear on any one area of the drive.

Similarly, early SSDs did not have the garbage-collection algorithms that are now standard in modern drives, which reclaim unused space on the drive to improve performance. These and other advanced features were gradually added to SSD firmware as the technology matured and the demands on SSDs increased.

Today, SSD firmware is a crucial component of modern storage systems, providing numerous benefits over traditional hard-disk drives (HDDs), such as faster access to data, higher reliability, and lower power consumption. It also enables several advanced features, such as data protection, power management, and error correction, which are essential for maintaining the integrity and performance of the drive.

One of the main challenges in achieving high performance with SSDs is their tendency to become bogged down by random input/output (IO) operations (IO operations are tasks that involve reading or writing data from or to the SSD, such as when you save a file or load a program), which occurs when the drive receives a large number of small, random read and write requests. To address this issue, SSD firmware began to incorporate stream concepts, which involve grouping together related IO requests and processing them as a single, larger request. This can significantly improve the performance of the drive by reducing the number of small IO requests and allowing the drive to operate more efficiently.

Another important aspect of SSD firmware is IO determinism, which refers to the ability of the drive to consistently deliver predictable performance. In the early days of SSDs, the performance of the drive could vary greatly depending on the workload, leading to unpredictable and inconsistent results. Modern SSD firmware includes features such as host cache, which uses system memory to store frequently accessed data, allowing the drive to deliver more consistent and predictable performance.

In summary, the history of SSD firmware reflects the evolution of SSD technology itself. Starting with simple firmware that was primarily responsible for interfacing with the host system, it has gradually evolved to include a wide range of advanced capabilities that are critical for modern storage systems.

Summary

This chapter has discussed the history and evolution of SSD firmware. We have seen how firmware has evolved from a simple piece of software to a complex and sophisticated piece of technology. We have also seen how firmware has helped to improve the performance, reliability, and efficiency of SSDs.

The chapter has also discussed some of the challenges that SSD firmware faces today. One of the main challenges is the need to improve the performance of SSDs under random IO conditions. Another challenge is the need to improve the IO determinism of SSDs.

Despite these challenges, SSD firmware continues to evolve and improve. As SSD technology continues to develop, we can expect to see even more advanced features and capabilities in the future.

CHAPTER 4

Basics of Flash Memory

In this chapter, we will discuss different memory types and delve into the world of flash memory, exploring its different types and focusing on two primary types: NAND and NOR flash memory. We will discuss the architecture of NAND flash memory and its fundamental operations, including reading, writing, and erasing data. Understanding these basic operations is crucial to grasp how NAND flash memory functions and how it is utilized in solid-state drive (SSD) firmware. By the end of this chapter, you will have gained valuable insights into the basics of flash memory, enabling you to comprehend its architecture and the fundamental operations it supports.

Memory Types

Flash memory is a type of non-volatile memory that is used in a variety of electronic devices, including SSDs. Non-volatile memory can retain data even when the power is turned off, making it ideal for storing important information.

There are several different types of flash memory available, including NOR and NAND, as you can see in Figure 4-1.

© Gopi Kuppan Thirumalai 2023
G. Kuppan Thirumalai, *A Beginner's Guide to SSD Firmware*,
https://doi.org/10.1007/978-1-4842-9888-6_4

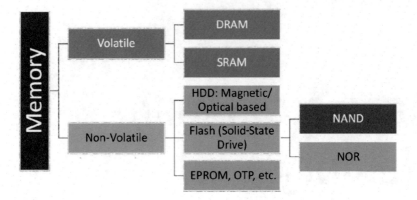

Figure 4-1. *Memory types*

NOR Flash Memory

NOR flash memory is capable of random access, meaning that data can be read or written to any location on the memory chip. It is commonly used in devices that require fast access to small amounts of data. It is possible to read/write one byte of data at a time. Erase operation is in sector wise. NOR flash memory is less dense, meaning it consumes more physical area and costs more than NAND flash memory.

Characteristics of NOR Flash Memory

The following are characteristics of NOR flash memory:

- Cost per bit is high.

- Code execution is easy.

- Capacity is low.

- Write speed is slower.

- Read speed is faster.

- Power consumption on standby is low.

NOR Memory Architecture

Take a look at the NOR memory architecture in Figure 4-2.

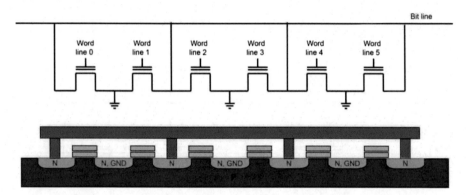

Figure 4-2. *NOR memory architecture*
Source: Wikipedia

NOR memory is a type of flash memory that uses NOR gates to store data. The gates are arranged in a grid, with each gate storing a single bit of data. The grid is divided into words, with each word containing a fixed number of bits.

To read data from NOR memory, the controller sends a `read` command to the memory. The memory then transfers the data from the selected word to the controller.

To write data to NOR memory, the controller sends a `write` command to the memory. The memory then writes the new data to the selected word.

NAND Flash Memory

NAND flash memory, however, is a type of flash memory that is optimized for high-capacity storage and fast data transfer. It is commonly used in SSDs and other storage devices, such as USB drives and memory cards. NAND memory is made up of tiny transistors that are arranged in a

grid and can be used to store data in the form of bits (0s and 1s). It is
fast and efficient, making it ideal for use in SSDs, and it is also relatively
inexpensive and widely available.

NAND Memory Architecture

Take a look at the NAND memory architecture in Figure 4-3.

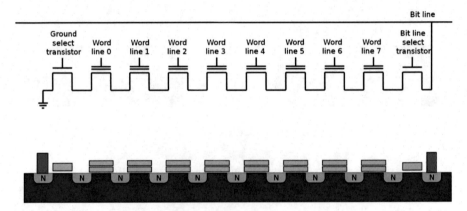

Figure 4-3. *NAND memory architecture*
Source: Wikipedia

NAND memory is a type of flash memory that uses floating-gate
transistors to store data. The transistors are arranged in a grid, with each
transistor storing a single bit of data. The grid is divided into pages, with
each page containing a fixed number of bits.

To read data from NAND memory, the controller sends a read
command to the memory. The memory then transfers the data from the
selected page to the controller.

To write data to NAND memory, the controller sends a write
command to the memory. The memory then erases the selected page and
writes the new data to the page.

Similarities

NAND and NOR memory are both types of flash memory. They both use transistors to store data, and they both have a grid-like structure.

Differences

The main difference between NAND and NOR memory is the way that they store data. NAND memory uses floating-gate transistors, while NOR memory uses NOR gates. This difference in the way that they store data affects the performance and the features of the two types of memory.

NAND memory is generally faster than NOR memory, but it is also more expensive. NAND memory is also more durable than NOR memory.

NOR memory is slower than NAND memory, but it is also less expensive. NOR memory is also easier to program than NAND memory.

A Flash Memory Cell

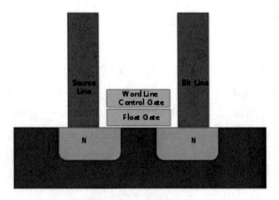

Figure 4-4. *A flash memory cell*

Flash memory, which is used in SSDs, combines the characteristics of ROM (read-only memory) and RAM (random access memory). It can retain information even when there is no power, like ROM, and it can be repeatedly erased and rewritten, like RAM. This is made possible through the use of a special type of transistor in flash memory.

Let's break down how it works in a simplified manner, as follows:

1. Typical Transistors: In typical memory transistors, there are three connections: source, drain, and gate. The source is where electricity enters, the drain is where it exits, and the gate controls the flow. When the gate is closed, no current can flow, turning the transistor off and storing a zero (0). When the gate is open, power flows through, activating the transistor and storing a one (1).

2. Limitations of Typical Transistors: However, a typical transistor cannot remember its state when the power is switched off. When power is turned back on, it's difficult to determine whether the transistor was on or off before the power was removed.

3. Flash Memory Transistors: Flash memory transistors have an additional connection called a floating gate. This floating gate is placed on top of the main gate. When the gate is open, electricity seeps through the first gate and remains trapped between the first and second gates, even when the power is off. Refer to Figure 4-5.

4. Retaining Information: The floating gate in flash memory allows it to remember its state even when the power is off. If you try to push current

through the transistor, the stored energy prevents
it, representing a zero. Clearing the stored energy
allows the current to flow, representing a one.
This way, the flash transistor retains information
regardless of whether the power is on or off.

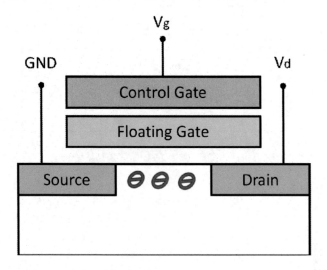

Figure 4-5. *Floating gate NMOS transistor*

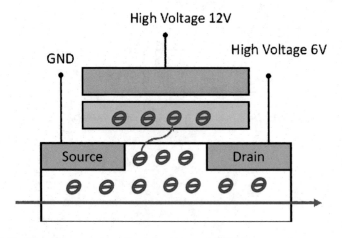

Figure 4-6. *Programming floating gate NMOS transistor*

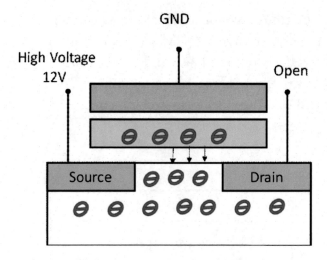

Figure 4-7. *Erasing floating gate NMOS transistor*

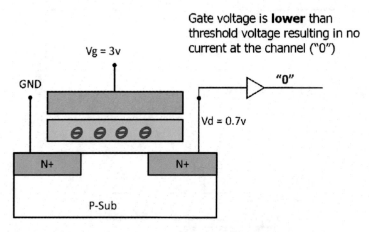

Figure 4-8. *Reading floating gate NMOS transistor*

Table 4-1. *Cell Node Voltages Required in Different Memory Operations*

Operation	Gate	Drain	Source	Bulk
Read	4.5	SA	0	0
Program	8.0	5.0	0	0
Erase	-8.0	Float	8.0	8.0

NAND Memory Organization

- The package is the memory chip, which contains one or more dies.

- The die is the smallest unit that can independently execute commands and report status.

- Each die contains one or more planes. Identical, concurrent operations can take place on each plane, although with some restrictions.

- Each plane contains a number of blocks, which are the smallest unit that can be erased. Remember that, as it's really important.

- Each block contains a number of pages, which are the smallest unit that can be programmed.

Addressing

It is NAND memory addressing. How physical nand can be addressed or accessed by Firmware.

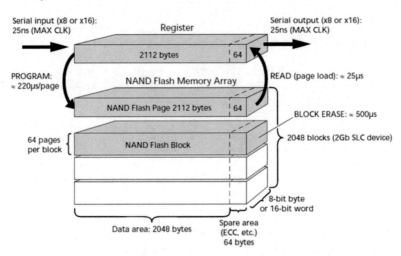

Figure 4-9. *The organizational structure of a NAND flash device Source: Micron Technology Inc.*

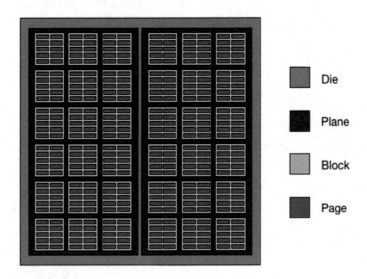

Figure 4-10. *NAND flash die layout Source: AnandTech*

Erase

In a flash memory device, the `erase` operation is responsible for changing the state of a cell from "0" to "1" by removing electrons from the floating gate. It is important to note that a single cell cannot be directly changed from "1" to "0"; instead, the `erase` operation must be performed on a block-by-block basis. This means that before new data can be written to a block (through the programming process), the block must first be erased to ensure that it is empty. It is worth noting that the `erase` operation typically has a longer latency than the `read` and `program` operations, meaning it can take longer to complete. For example, the read, program, and erase latencies for a Micron 8 GB flash chip are 25 μs, 220 μs, and 1500 μs, respectively. As a result, the `erase` operation can be a performance bottleneck in NAND flash memories, and various firmware algorithms have been developed to minimize the impact of the long erase latency on overall performance.

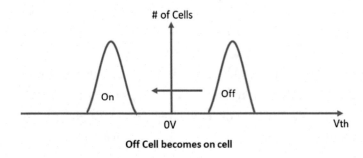

Figure 4-11. *Erase level Vth distribution*

Write

The `program` operation is performed on a page level. This means that the operation targets a specific page of memory on the drive. When the controller of the SSD requests a program operation on the NAND device, it specifies the chip select (CE) and provides the row address of the page

25

to be targeted. The controller then transfers the data to be programmed to the NAND device and sends a final `program` command to complete the operation.

It is important to note that a page on an SSD cannot be written more than once without first performing an `erase` operation. This is because an `erase` operation is required to clear the page of any existing data before new data can be written to it. As a result, every time a `program` operation is performed on a page, it must be preceded by an `erase` operation. This ensures that the page is ready to accept new data and that the `program` operation is successful.

It is also important to say that pages need to be written in consecutive order within the block; page number 0 is to be written first followed by page 1. Writing out of sequence is not allowed, as violating this rule aggravates the bit error rate. A single block does not need to be written all at once. That is, a block can be written with pages from 0 to 11, and later on with pages from 12 to 32, for example. Generally, pages need to be written as a whole at once, though some memories support so-called *partial page programming*, which allows a subpage of 512 bytes + correlated spare area to be written.

The data to be written will be provided by the host or result from firmware internal data management. Firmware first transfers the data from cache to the NAND internal cache register. Once the data transfer is completed the programming should start; i.e., writing to actual NAND cells.

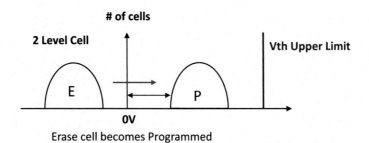

Figure 4-12. *Program level Vth distribution*

Read

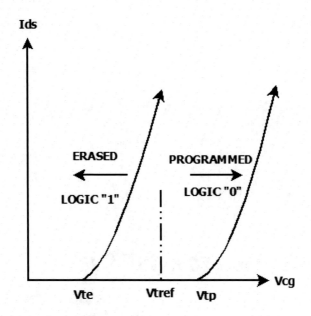

Figure 4-13. *Read sensing graph*

From the perspective of the NAND chips themselves, the read operation involves activating the appropriate word line to select the desired page of cells, and then reading the data stored in those cells by sensing the voltage levels on the bit lines. The NAND chips are organized into blocks, which are further divided into pages. Each page stores a fixed amount of data, typically 4 KB to 16 KB (or more), depending on the specific NAND device.

To read a specific page, the controller must first locate the block that contains the page and then activate the appropriate word line to select the page within that block. The read operation is typically performed by the SSD's controller, which uses firmware to manage the communication with the NAND chips and handle the necessary data transfer and error correction. The firmware is responsible for optimizing the read performance by minimizing the number of accesses required and maximizing the data transfer rate.

Table 4-2. *NAND Basic Operations Timings*

Operation	Area	Time (Example)
Erase	Block	500 us
Write	Page	220 us
Read	Page	25 us

Program/Erase Cycle (P/E Cycle)

The program/erase (P/E) cycle is a fundamental aspect of NAND flash memory, which is commonly used in SSDs. NAND flash memory works by storing data in cells that are grouped into blocks. Each cell can store a single bit of data, and a group of cells is needed to store a larger amount of data. To write new data to a cell, the cell must first be erased, which is done by applying a high voltage to the cell. As we already explained, this process is known as the erase cycle.

Once the cell has been erased, new data can be written to it using a process called programming, which involves applying a lower voltage to the cell. The process of writing new data to a cell by first erasing it and then programming it with new data is known as the P/E cycle. The P/E cycle is a key factor in the endurance of NAND flash memory, as the erase cycle can cause wear on the cells over time. As a result, NAND flash memory has a limited number of P/E cycles that it can withstand before it begins to degrade. This is known as the endurance of the memory.

To extend the endurance of NAND flash memory, it is important to minimize the number of P/E cycles that the memory undergoes. One way to do this is to use the TRIM command, which allows the operating system to inform the SSD which data blocks are no longer in use and can be erased. This can reduce the number of P/E cycles by eliminating the need to move invalid data during the garbage-collection process, which is an internal SSD housekeeping operation that manages and maintains available storage space.

The number of bits that can be stored in each cell of a NAND flash memory drive can also affect the maximum number of program/erase (P/E) cycles that the drive can support. Table 4-3 provides an overview of the different types of NAND cells based on the number of bits they can store.

Table 4-3. *PEC Cycle Based on NAND Cell Type*

Cell type	Bits per cell	Supported P/E cycles
Single-level cell (SLC)	1	100,000
Multi-level cell (MLC)	2	10,000 - 30,000
Triple-level cell (TLC)	3	3,000 - 5,000
Quad-level cell (QLC)	4	1,000 - 3,000

As the number of bits per cell increases, the number of supported P/E cycles tends to decrease. Single-level cell (SLC) NAND, which can store one bit per cell, generally has the highest endurance, while quad-level cell (QLC) NAND, which can store four bits per cell, has the lowest endurance. It is important to consider the endurance of an SSD when selecting a drive, as a drive with a lower endurance may not be suitable for use in cases that involve a high number of P/E cycles.

Summary

This chapter has discussed the basics of flash memory, including its different types, architecture, and fundamental operations. We have seen how NAND flash memory works and how it is used in SSDs. We have also seen the different types of operations that can be performed on NAND flash memory, such as erase, program, and read. We have also discussed the P/E cycle, which is a key factor in the endurance of NAND flash memory.

CHAPTER 5

3D Vertical NAND

Now, welcome to the exciting world of 3D vertical NAND! In this chapter, we will cover a cutting-edge technology that has revolutionized the way we store data. 3D vertical NAND is a remarkable advancement in NAND flash memory, allowing us to stack memory cells vertically to increase storage capacity and performance significantly.

You might be wondering how this technology works and what makes it so special. We will walk through the basics of 3D vertical NAND, explaining its unique architecture and how it overcomes the limitations of traditional 2D planar NAND. You'll discover the advantages and benefits of this innovative technology, along with its real-world applications and the impact it has on various industries.

By the end of this chapter, you will have a clear understanding of how 3D vertical NAND works and how it has transformed data storage, making it a technology crucial to modern electronic devices. So, let's dive in and explore the fascinating world of 3D vertical NAND!

Evolution of 3D Vertical NAND Technology

The rapid growth in data traffic globally is pushing the boundaries of NAND flash memory technology. The industry-standard 2D planar NAND technology has inherent limitations when it comes to expanding storage capacity without compromising performance and reliability. This has created a need for innovative solutions to meet the increasing demands for data storage.

© Gopi Kuppan Thirumalai 2023
G. Kuppan Thirumalai, *A Beginner's Guide to SSD Firmware*,
https://doi.org/10.1007/978-1-4842-9888-6_5

To address these challenges, the industry has introduced a groundbreaking approach known as 3D vertical NAND (V-NAND) flash memory technology. This innovation has revolutionized the design and architecture of NAND flash memory by stacking memory cells vertically in a three-dimensional structure, as opposed to the traditional two-dimensional planar arrangement. This vertical stacking allows for the creation of multiple layers of memory cells, resulting in significantly higher memory capacities (Figure 5-1).

By adopting a 3D V-NAND structure, the industry has overcome the limitations associated with capacity expansion in 2D planar NAND technology. This vertical stacking not only enables higher storage densities but also eliminates performance and reliability issues caused by capacity constraints. With more memory cells packed into each chip, the industry has achieved remarkable advancements in storage capacity while maintaining or even enhancing performance and reliability characteristics.

The vertical stacking of memory cells in 3D V-NAND technology offers several advantages. First, it allows for increased memory capacity within a smaller physical footprint, which is particularly beneficial in applications where space is a constraint. Additionally, the three-dimensional structure enables better control of electrical properties, resulting in improved performance and endurance.

This innovation in flash memory technology has had a significant impact on the storage industry, enabling the development of high-capacity solid-state drives (SSDs) that can handle the ever-growing volumes of data. The adoption of 3D V-NAND technology has facilitated advancements in areas such as cloud computing, data centers, mobile devices, and other storage-intensive applications.

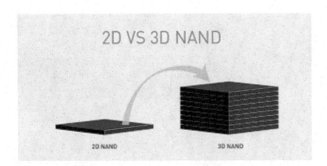

Figure 5-1. *2D vs. 3D NAND comparison block diagram*

Unlocking New Possibilities with Vertical NAND Architecture

Figure 5-2 compares the storage density of 2D planar NAND and 3D V-NAND flash memory. As shown, 3D V-NAND can achieve up to 10x greater storage density than 2D planar NAND. This is because 3D V-NAND stacks memory cells vertically on top of each other, while 2D planar NAND stacks memory cells horizontally on a silicon wafer.

The higher storage density of 3D V-NAND allows for larger capacity NAND chips to be produced. This has made it possible to create NAND flash memory devices such as solid-state drives (SSDs) and USB flash drives with capacities of several terabytes.

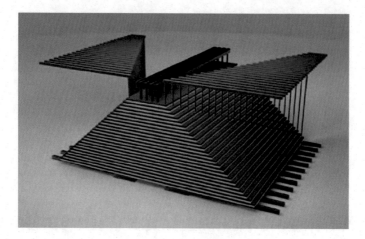

Figure 5-2. *Bird's-eye view of the V-NAND structure*

In the pursuit of fitting more memory cells into a smaller space, the limitations of 2D planar NAND flash memory become evident. The shrinking size makes it challenging for light to penetrate the mask and transfer the desired pattern onto the photoresist, ultimately hindering the patterning process. This inherent limitation restricts the widespread use of 2D planar NAND flash memory in today's demanding memory landscape.

However, 3D V-NAND overcomes these patterning limitations by adopting a vertical architecture. Unlike the close proximity of cells in 2D planar NAND, 3D V-NAND creates a wider gap between each cell, enabling efficient patterning. While the cell-to-cell spacing in traditional planar NAND typically ranges from 15 to 16 nanometers (nm), 3D V-NAND offers an impressive 30nm to 40nm of space between cells, revolutionizing NAND flash technology.

This vertical architecture has opened new doors for memory advancement, allowing for higher capacities and enhanced performance. By overcoming the constraints of patterning, 3D V-NAND flash memory has become a game-changer in the industry, meeting the demands of today's memory-intensive applications.

2D NAND

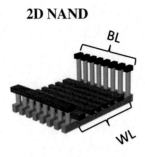

3D NAND

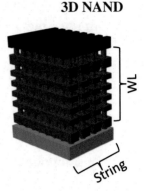

Figure 5-3. *2D planar NAND vs. 3D Vertical NAND*

Advantages of 3D Vertical NAND

3D vertical NAND has several advantages over traditional planar NAND, as follows:

    a.   Higher Storage Capacities: The vertical stacking of memory cells enables significant increases in storage capacities. With more layers of cells, 3D V-NAND offers the potential for greater memory densities, allowing for storage devices with larger capacities.

    b.   Improved Performance: 3D V-NAND can deliver enhanced read and write speeds compared to 2D planar NAND. The vertical structure reduces the distance that signals need to travel, resulting in faster data access and transfer rates.

35

c.   Enhanced Endurance: Vertical NAND architecture improves the endurance of the memory cells. The increased space between cells reduces interference, leading to improved reliability and longevity.

d.   Energy Efficiency: 3D V-NAND technology offers improved energy efficiency, allowing for longer battery life in portable devices and reduced power consumption in data centers.

Applications of 3D Vertical NAND

The advantages offered by 3D vertical NAND make it well suited for various applications, including the following:

a.   Solid-State Drives (SSDs): SSDs equipped with 3D V-NAND deliver high-speed data storage and retrieval, making them ideal for use in laptops, desktops, and enterprise storage solutions. The increased storage capacity enables SSDs to meet the demands of modern data-intensive applications.

b.   Mobile Devices: Smartphones, tablets, and other portable devices benefit from the compact size and high storage capacities of 3D V-NAND. These devices require reliable and fast storage solutions to handle multimedia content, applications, and operating systems.

c.   Data Centers and Cloud Computing: The scalability and performance of 3D V-NAND make it a valuable technology for data centers and cloud computing environments. The increased storage densities and improved reliability contribute to efficient data management and faster processing speeds.

Understanding 3D Vertical NAND Architecture

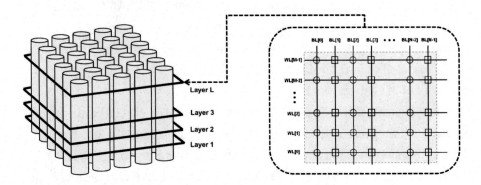

Figure 5-4. *3D vertical NAND layered architecture*

The unique architecture of 3D vertical NAND involves intricate vertical cell stacking and layering, which enables higher storage density and better performance. A block consists of vertically stacked layers of NAND flash cells, each consisting of grid of cells connected by Wordlines (WLs) and Bit Lines (BLs).

The vertical cell stacking approach ensures that more memory cells can be packed in a smaller space. This is achieved by placing multiple layers of memory cells on top of each other, making the most efficient use of available silicon area.

Each memory cell in 3D vertical NAND still consists of a transistor and a floating gate, just like in traditional NAND flash memory. However, the arrangement of these components is optimized for vertical stacking.

Layers and Pages

A 3D vertical NAND chip is composed of multiple layers, and each layer is divided into pages. Within a layer, pages are accessed individually for read and write operations. The vertical stacking of pages allows for greater memory capacity without increasing the chip's physical size.

Charge Trapping Technology

In 3D vertical NAND, memory cells use a charge trapping technology, unlike the floating-gate technology found in traditional NAND. Charge trapping stores charge in a non-conductive layer, preventing data loss due to electron leakage, which was a challenge in floating-gate technology. This enhanced data retention capability contributes to the reliability and longevity of 3D vertical NAND.

The 3D vertical NAND cell (also known as a V-NAND cell) is a type of NAND flash memory cell that is stacked vertically on top of other NAND flash memory cells. This allows for significantly greater storage density than traditional 2D planar NAND cells, which are stacked horizontally on a silicon wafer.

As shown in Figure 5-5, the 3D vertical NAND cell consists of three main components:

> The charge storage film: This layer is made of a material that can trap electrons. The number of electrons trapped in this layer determines the state of the cell (0 or 1).

> The control gate: This gate is used to control the flow of electrons into and out of the charge trap layer.

> The channel layer: This layer is made of a semiconducting material that allows electrons to flow through it.

3D Vertical NAND Cell

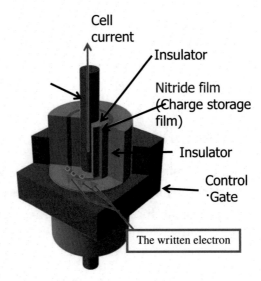

Information stored in nitride film (Charge Trap: insulator)

Cell current (Ic)

Figure 5-5. *3D NAND cell*

To store a bit of data in a 3D vertical NAND cell, a voltage is applied to the control gate. This causes electrons to flow into or out of the charge trap layer, depending on the desired state of the cell. Once the desired state has been achieved, the voltage is removed and the electrons are trapped in the charge trap layer.

The 3D vertical NAND cell is a highly efficient way to store data. It offers significantly greater storage density than traditional 2D planar NAND cells, while also being more energy-efficient. This makes it the ideal choice for a wide range of applications, including solid-state drives (SSDs), USB flash drives, and mobile devices.

Bit Line and Word Line Architecture

The bit lines and word lines form the essential structure of 3D vertical NAND. Bit lines run vertically through all layers, connecting the memory cells within a column. Word lines, however, run horizontally, connecting the memory cells across a row in each layer.

Control and Decoding Circuits

Control and decoding circuits are responsible for managing the flow of data in 3D vertical NAND. These circuits decode address inputs, control the selection of memory cells during read and write operations, and handle other essential functionalities.

Memory Cell Size and Density in 3D Vertical NAND Flash Memory Technology

3D vertical NAND (V-NAND) flash memory technology is a type of non-volatile memory that stacks memory cells vertically to increase storage density and capacity. One of the factors that affects the density and capacity of V-NAND chips is the size of the memory cells. As technology advances, manufacturers can reduce the size of the memory cells to fit more of them in a given area, resulting in higher density and larger capacity NAND chips. However, shrinking the cell size also poses some challenges, such as increased interference and reduced reliability. To overcome these challenges, V-NAND technology uses techniques such as charge trap flash (CTF) and tunnel field-effect transistor (TFET) to improve the performance and endurance of the memory cells. Moreover, V-NAND technology can also use different levels of charge to store multiple bits per cell, such as quad-level cell (QLC) or even higher, to further increase the storage capacity of NAND chips.

Understanding NAND Cell Types Supported: SLC, MLC, and TLC (QLC)

There are different types of memory cells, including SLC (single-level cell), MLC (multi-level cell), and TLC (triple-level cell). Each cell type comes with its own characteristics, influencing how data is stored, accessed, and managed. We'll discuss the principles of reading, writing, and erasing data from 3D vertical NAND flash.

SLC

3D vertical NAND SLC Vth distribution refers to the distribution of threshold voltages (Vth) of the memory cells in a 3D vertical NAND SLC flash memory device. Vth is a critical parameter that determines the performance and reliability of a NAND flash memory device. A narrow Vth distribution is desirable, as it indicates that all of the memory cells have similar Vth values. This makes it easier to read and write data to the memory cells, and it also reduces the risk of errors.

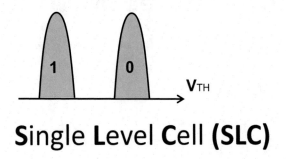

Figure 5-6. *3D vertical NAND SLC Vth distribution*

- 2 States (1 Erase + 1 Program) = 1 bit of information per cell

41

MLC

3D vertical NAND MLC Vth distribution refers to the distribution of threshold voltages (Vth) of the memory cells in a 3D vertical NAND MLC flash memory device. MLC NAND flash memory devices can store more than one bit (2-4) of data per memory cell, which requires a wider Vth range than SLC NAND flash memory devices. However, a narrow Vth distribution is still desirable for MLC NAND flash memory devices, as it improves performance and reliability.

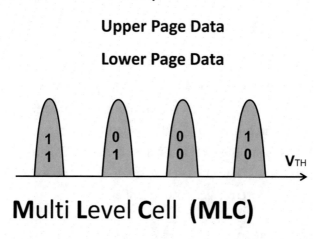

Figure 5-7. *3D vertical NAND MLC Vth distribution*

- 4 States (1 Erase + 3 Program)

  = 2 bits of information per cell

  = 2x capacity of SLC!

TLC

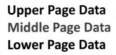

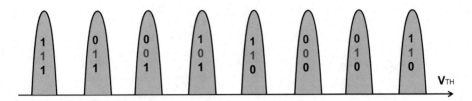

Triple Level Cell (TLC)

Figure 5-8. *3D vertical NAND TLC Vth distribution*

8 States (1 Erase + 7 Program)

> = 3 bits of information per cell
>
> = 1.5x capacity of MLC
>
> = 3.0x capacity of SLC

Read and Write Operations in 3D Vertical NAND

3D vertical NAND exhibits remarkable read and write operations owing to its unique vertical architecture. During a read operation, the control gate voltage is adjusted, allowing the flow of current through the memory cell. The resulting current state is then sensed to determine the stored data. The vertical stacking of memory cells enables faster read operations by reducing the distance the current needs to travel, resulting in reduced read latency.

43

Write operations in 3D vertical NAND involve programming the memory cell to store data. The voltage applied to the control gate elevates the electron energy in the floating gate, causing the charge to be trapped, representing either a 0 or 1. The vertical architecture enhances write performance by reducing the parasitic capacitance between memory cells, enabling faster and more efficient write operations.

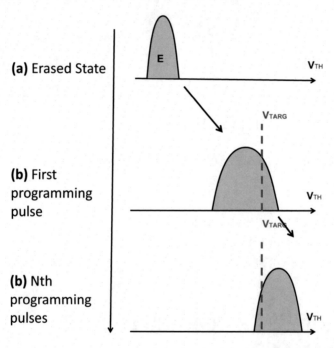

Figure 5-9. *3D vertical NAND SLC incremental programming pulse*

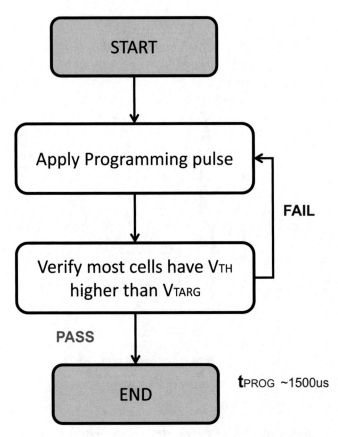

Figure 5-10. *3D vertical NAND SLC incremental programming pulse flow chart*

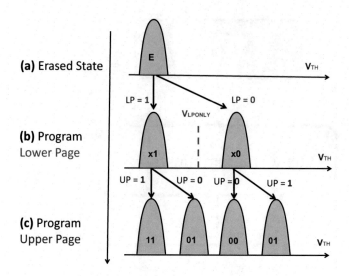

Figure 5-11. *3D vertical NAND MLC program sequence*

- Data is programmed to the device one page at a time.

- The cells are either left in the erased state or programmed to an intermediate state, depending on the lower page data.

- An intermediate read determines the previously programmed lower page data, and the cell distribution for the WL is "finalized" using the upper page data.

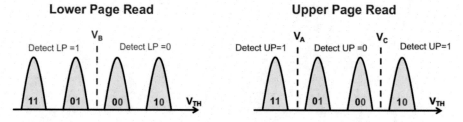

Figure 5-12. *Reading data from 3D vertical NAND MLC*

- Lower page can be read using a single read voltage (VB).

- Upper page can be read using a pair of read voltages (VA,VC).

- A page read (from NAND cell to NAND cache) typically takes up to 100us.

Erasing MLC 3D vertical NAND block

Erasing an MLC 3D vertical NAND block is the process of resetting all of the memory cells in the block to the same state. This is done by applying a high voltage to the block. The high voltage causes electrons to flow out of the charge trap layers in the memory cells, erasing the data.

Erasing MLC 3D vertical NAND blocks is more complex than erasing SLC NAND blocks because of the wider Vth range of MLC memory cells. To ensure that all of the memory cells in an MLC block are properly erased, the erase voltage must be carefully controlled.

There are a number of different methods for erasing MLC 3D vertical NAND blocks. One common method is to use a partial erase scheme. In a partial erase scheme, the erase voltage is gradually increased until all of the memory cells in the block are erased. This method is more energy-efficient than erasing the block at a single high voltage, but it takes longer.

Another method for erasing MLC 3D vertical NAND blocks is to use a full erase scheme. In a full erase scheme, the erase voltage is set to a high value for a fixed period of time. This method is faster than a partial erase scheme, but it consumes more energy.

The best method for erasing MLC 3D vertical NAND blocks depends on the specific application. For example, applications that require high performance may be willing to sacrifice some energy efficiency in order to achieve faster erase times.

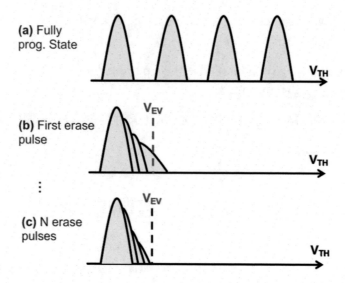

Figure 5-13. *Erasing MLC 3D vertical NAND block*

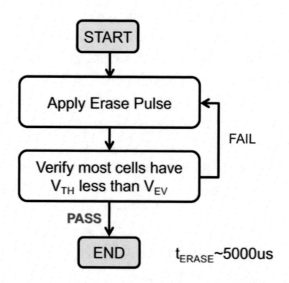

Figure 5-14. *Flow Diagram for 3D vertical NAND block erase MLC*

Endurance and Data Retention Capabilities

Endurance and data retention are crucial aspects of NAND flash memory. 3D vertical NAND excels in both areas due to its improved memory cell design and materials. The vertical structure reduces crosstalk and interference between memory cells, leading to improved data-retention capabilities. As a result, data stored in 3D vertical NAND remains intact for longer periods, even under challenging conditions.

Additionally, the vertical stacking design contributes to enhanced endurance by reducing wear on individual memory cells. This translates to a higher number of program-erase cycles before memory cell degradation, making 3D vertical NAND a reliable choice for data-intensive applications that require frequent read and write operations.

Speed and Efficiency Compared to 2D Planar NAND

Compared to traditional 2D planar NAND, 3D vertical NAND offers notable speed and efficiency advantages. The vertical stacking of memory cells results in shorter electrical pathways, reducing data access times and improving overall system performance.

With faster read and write operations, 3D vertical NAND outperforms 2D planar NAND in data access speed, making it an excellent choice for applications requiring real-time data processing. Moreover, the improved efficiency of 3D vertical NAND contributes to lower power consumption, leading to energy savings and prolonged battery life in portable devices.

Advancements in Storage Capacity with 3D Vertical NAND

One of the most significant achievements of 3D vertical NAND is the substantial advancement in storage capacity. The vertical cell stacking allows for a more efficient use of space, enabling the integration of multiple memory-cell layers within the same footprint.

As a result, 3D vertical NAND-based data storage solutions can achieve much higher capacities compared to traditional 2D planar NAND devices. This breakthrough has enabled the development of solid-state drives (SSDs) and memory modules with unprecedented storage capabilities, catering to the ever-growing demands of data-intensive applications.

Summary

With this very brief chapter on 3D Vertical NAND, we have covered the basics only. As you delve into this exciting field of advanced memory technology, you will gain a deeper understanding of how 3D vertical NAND is revolutionizing data storage and setting the stage for future innovations in the semiconductor industry. As engineers and developers, your expertise in harnessing the capabilities of 3D vertical NAND will be instrumental in creating next-generation storage solutions that cater to the evolving needs of our data-driven world. Embrace the power of 3D vertical NAND and unlock the endless possibilities it holds for shaping the future of storage technology from here.

CHAPTER 6

Basic Understanding of NAND Flash Interface

In this chapter, we will examine the fundamental aspects of NAND flash memory and explore how it can be effectively utilized in embedded systems and be made into a product. We will delve into the essential aspects of NAND flash communication, including the commands it supports, data transfer procedures, commands, response packet information, and much more. By understanding the key features of NAND flash, engineers can leverage its power, density, and cost advantages to create efficient and reliable subsystems for various applications, including solid-state drives (SSDs), mobile phones, flash memory cards, USB flash drives, and audio/video players.

NAND flash supports a set of specific commands that facilitate various operations, such as read, write, erase, and status checking. We will thoroughly examine each command, its purpose, and the relevant response packet information. A clear understanding of these commands is crucial for effectively managing data access and storage in NAND flash memory.

© Gopi Kuppan Thirumalai 2023
G. Kuppan Thirumalai, *A Beginner's Guide to SSD Firmware*,
https://doi.org/10.1007/978-1-4842-9888-6_6

Basic NAND IO Interfacing Pin Details

Table 6-1. *NAND IO Interfacing Pin Details*

PIN	Description
CE#	Chip enable CE# serves as the chip enable signal for the NAND flash device. When CE# is not asserted (held high), the NAND flash remains in standby mode and does not respond to any control signals. Activating CE# allows the device to operate and respond to commands.
WE#	Write enable WE# is responsible for clocking data, address, or commands into the NAND flash device. When WE# is low, data, addresses, or commands are written to the device, and the relevant information is latched into the internal registers.
RE#	Read enable RE# is used to enable the output data buffers of the NAND flash device. When RE# is low, data from the device's internal memory cells is available on the data bus for read operations.
CLE	Command latch enable CLE is a control signal used to latch commands and addresses into the NAND flash device. When CLE is set to a high state, commands are latched into the command register on the rising edge of the WE# signal.
ALE	Address latch enable When ALE is high, addresses are latched into the NAND flash address register on the rising edge of the WE# signal.
I/O[7:0]	Data bus (I/O[15:0} for x16 parts) The data bus pins (DQ pins) are used for bidirectional data transfer between the NAND flash device and the host system. During write operations, the host inputs command, address, and data to the NAND flash through these pins. During read operations, the device outputs data to the host using the same pins.

(*continued*)

Table 6-1. (*continued*)

PIN	Description
WP#	Write protect WP# is a write protect signal that can be used to block any program and erase operations on the flash array. When WP# is active low, write operations are prevented, providing a hardware-based write protection mechanism.
R/B#	Ready/busy The R/B# signal indicates the status of the NAND flash device. If the device is busy with an erase, program, or read operation, the R/B# signal is asserted low. It is an open drain signal and requires a pull-up resistor to ensure proper signal levels

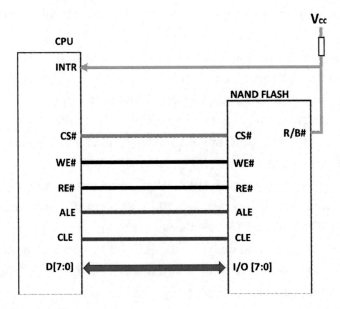

Figure 6-1. *Basic CPU NAND interconnect*

NAND Flash Interface Basics

The NAND flash memory interface is an essential aspect of hardware design when integrating NAND into a system. In a NAND flash memory interface, data is transferred into or out of the NAND flash register in 8- or 16-bit chunks at a time. During a program operation, the data to be programmed is loaded into the data register on the rising edge of the write enable (WE#) signal. To enable random access to data or movement within the register, special commands are used, such as RANDOM DATA INPUT and READ FOR INTERNAL DATA MOVE.

When it comes to outputting data from the data register, the read enable (RE#) signal is employed. Activating RE# allows the current data to be output, and the register then increments to the next location, enabling sequential data retrieval.

For seamless integration with other memory types, NAND flash utilizes the chip enable (CE#) and read enable (RE#) signals in combination. When CE# or RE# are not asserted LOW, the output buffers are set to a tri-state mode, allowing NAND flash to share the data bus with other memory types, like NOR Flash, SRAM, or DRAM. This characteristic is known as "chip enable don't care."

NAND flash operations are initiated by issuing a command cycle, where the command is placed on I/O[7:0], CE# is set LOW, and command latch enable (CLE) is set HIGH. A WE# clock is then used to clock the commands, addresses, and data into the NAND flash device on the rising edge of WE#. It's essential to understand this command-driven approach to efficiently manage data access and system control.

Most commands require a series of address cycles followed by a second command cycle. However, it's important to note that new commands should not be issued while the NAND flash device is busy with ongoing operations. The RESET and READ STATUS commands are exceptions to this rule and can be issued even when the device is busy.

The NAND flash memory interface involves the communication protocol used to read, write, and erase data from the NAND device. The most common NAND flash interfaces used in consumer electronics and computing devices are the Open NAND Flash Interface (ONFI) and Toggle Mode Interface.

Open NAND Flash Interface (ONFI)

ONFI is an industry-standard interface for NAND flash memory that allows for faster data transfer rates and improved compatibility between NAND devices and NAND controllers. It defines a set of commands and timing requirements that facilitate communication between the controller and the NAND flash memory. ONFI supports both asynchronous and synchronous data transfer modes.

In asynchronous mode, the data transfer is initiated by the controller, and the NAND flash memory responds accordingly. In synchronous mode, the data transfer is synchronized to the system clock, allowing for higher data transfer rates.

Toggle Mode Interface

Toggle Mode Interface is another high-speed interface commonly used in NAND flash memory. It provides faster data transfer rates compared to traditional interfaces. Toggle Mode Interface employs a bidirectional data bus and a separate command/address bus to enable faster read and write operations.

Toggle Mode Interface has two versions, namely, Toggle Mode 1.0 and Toggle Mode 2.0. Toggle Mode 2.0 offers higher data transfer rates and improved performance compared to Toggle Mode 1.0.

Toggle 2.0 is a high-performance flash memory interface that supports data read and write operations using bidirectional. It implements double data rate (DDR) without a clock, and is compatible with the functions and commands supported by conventional flash memory (i.e., SDR flash memory). Toggle 2.0 flash memory provides high data transfer rates based on the high-speed Toggle DDR interface and saves power by using separated DQ voltage.

Toggle DDR 2.0 flash memory supports an interface speed of up to 200 MHz (400 Mbps), which is more than ten times faster than the data transfer rate offered by SDR flash memory (40 Mbps). Toggle DDR flash memory transfers data at high speed using data strobe (DQS), which behaves as a clock. However, DQS is only used when data is transferred so as to optimize power consumption.

Toggle DDR flash memory is the most appropriate choice for applications that require high-capacity and high-performance flash memory.

Command Cycles for NAND Flash Operations

The NAND flash memory employs a set of basic command sequences for its operation. The addresses are multiplexed into eight I/Os, and all commands, addresses, and data are written through DQ [7:0] pins by bringing WE (write enable) low while CE (chip enable) is low. The data is latched on the rising edge of WE.

To facilitate the multiplexing of commands and addresses, NAND flash utilizes command latch enable (CLE) and address latch enable (ALE) signals. CLE is used to multiplex command data via the DQ[7:0] pins, while ALE is employed to multiplex address data via the same pins.

Commands that apply to a specific page or block typically have a second command, while commands that apply to a target have only a first command. These basic command sets enable efficient control and access to specific operations within the NAND flash memory, ensuring reliable and fast data transfers.

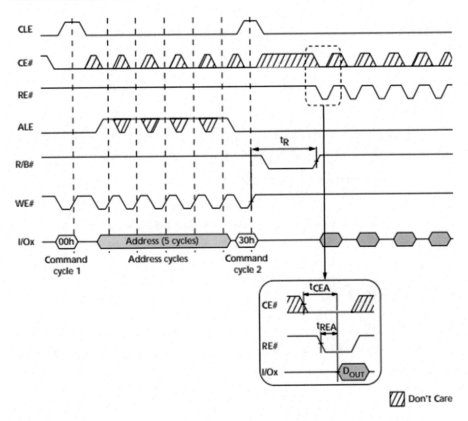

Figure 6-2. *Command cycles for NAND flash operations*

Addressing

In NAND flash memory, addressing involves two types: the column address and the row address. Understanding how these addresses work is essential to grasp how data is accessed and organized within the memory.

Column Address

The column address is used to access specific bytes within a page of the NAND flash memory. Think of it as the "byte offset" into the page, allowing the system to pinpoint the exact location of data within a page. Notably, for a DDR interface (double data rate), the least significant bit of the column address is always set to zero. This ensures that an even number of bytes is always transferred, promoting efficient data handling.

Row Address

The row address serves a broader purpose. It is used to address entire pages and blocks within the NAND flash memory. By utilizing the row address, the system can access specific pages or blocks as needed. When both the column and the row addresses are required, the column address is always issued first, followed by the row addresses in separate 8-bit address cycles.

Addressing Functions

Some operations only require row addresses, such as block erase. In such cases, the column addresses are not issued, streamlining the process for specific functions.

Address Cycle Order

When issuing both column and row addresses, the first address cycle always contains the least significant address bits, while the last address cycle contains the most significant address bits. This logical order ensures that the system can accurately interpret the address information.

Handling Unused Bits

In the most significant cycles of both the column and the row addresses, some bits may not be utilized for specific memory configurations. To maintain consistency, any unused bits in these cycles must be cleared to zero.

In addition to understanding the column and row addresses, there are certain constraints that the host must adhere to when accessing NAND flash memory to ensure proper and safe operation.

Address Limitations

A crucial consideration is that a firmware must not attempt to access an address of a page or block beyond the maximum page address or block address supported by the NAND flash memory. Accessing addresses beyond these limits can result in unintended behavior—data corruption.

Valid Address Range

Before performing any erase, read, or write operations, the host must verify that the target address falls within the valid address range of the NAND flash memory. The valid address range is determined by the maximum page and block addresses supported by the memory device.

Address Validation

The firmware in the SSD controller or the host system should include proper address validation mechanisms to ensure that any incoming address requests are within the valid range. If an invalid address is detected, the system should handle it gracefully, either by rejecting the request or by raising appropriate error flags.

By adhering to the address limitations, the firmware can prevent unintended consequences and ensure the stability and reliability of data operations on the NAND flash memory. Proper validation and error-handling mechanisms play a crucial role in safeguarding the integrity of data and the long-term health of the memory device.

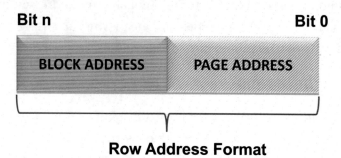

Figure 6-3. NAND row address format

Table 6-2. 2Gb SLC NAND Flash Addressing Scheme

Cycle	I/07	I/06	I/05	I/04	I/03	I/02	I/01	I/00
First	CA7	CA6	CA5	CA4	CA3	CA2	CA1	CA0
Second	LOW	LOW	LOW	LOW	CA11	CA10	CA9	CA8
Third	BA7	BA6	PA5	PA4	PA3	PA2	PA1	PA0
Fourth	BA15	BA14	BA13	BA12	BA11	BA10	BA9	BA8
Fifth	LOW	LOW	LOW	LOW	LOW	LOW	LOW	BA16

Notes: Block address concatenated with page address = actual page address.

CAx = Column Address

PAx = Page Address

BAx = Block Address

The page address and the block address, collectively, constitute the row address (and number of bits depends on the NAND die size)

The most significant address byte is the fifth cycle; the least significant address byte is the first cycle.

The addressing scheme for a 2Gb NAND flash device is represented in Table 6-2. When accessing specific data within the page, the first and second address cycles (or bytes) indicate the column address, defining the starting byte. For example, if the last column location is 2112, its address would be 08h in the second byte and 3Fh in the first byte. The page address within the block is determined by PA[5:0], while BA[16:6] identifies the block address.

In most PROGRAM and READ operations, the full 5-byte address is required to access data accurately. However, for operations that involve random data access within the page, only the first and second bytes (or cycles) are necessary. Meanwhile, when performing the BLOCK ERASE operation, only the three most significant bytes (third, fourth, and fifth) are utilized to select the block.

Table 6-3. *Command Cycles and Address Cycles*

Command	Command Cycle 1	Number of Address Cycles	Data Cycles Required 1	Command Cycle2	Valid During Busy
READ PAGE	00h	5	No	30h	No
READ PAGE CACHE SEQUENTIAL	31h	–	No	–	No
READ PAGE CACHE SEQUENTIAL LAST	3Fh	–	No	–	No
READ for INTERNAL DATA MOVE	00h	5	No	35h	No
RANDOM D ATA READ		05h	2	No	E0h
READ ID	90h	1	No	–	No
READ STATUS	70h	–	No	–	Yes

(continued)

Table 6-3. (*continued*)

Command	Command Cycle 1	Number of Address Cycles	Data Cycles Required 1	Command Cycle2	Valid During Busy
PROGRAM PAGE	80h	5	Yes	10h	No
PROGRAM PAGE CACHE	80h	5	Yes	15h	No
PROGRAM for INTERNAL DATA MOVE	85h	5	Optional	10h	No
RANDOM DATA INPUT	85h	2	Yes	–	No
ERASE BLOCK	60h	3	No	D0h	No
RESET	FFh	–	No	–	Yes

NAND Flash Commands

When any NAND flash command is issued, CE# and ALE must be LOW, CLE must be asserted, and write clocks (WE#) must be provided. When any NAND flash address is issued, CE# and CLE must be LOW, ALE must be asserted, and write clocks (WE#) must be provided. While the device is busy, only two commands can be issued: RESET and READ STATUS.

RESET Operation

The simplest NAND flash command is the RESET (FFh) command. The RESET command does not require an address or subsequent cycle(s). Simply assert CLE and issue a write clock with FFh on the data bus, and a RESET operation is performed. This RESET command must be issued immediately following power-up and prior to issuing any other command.

RESET is one of two commands that can be issued while the NAND flash device is busy. If the device is busy processing a previous command, issuing a RESET command aborts the previous operation. If the previous operation was an ERASE or PROGRAM command, issuing a RESET command aborts the command prematurely, and the desired operation does not complete. ERASE and PROGRAM can be time-consuming operations; issuing the RESET command makes it possible to abort either and reissue the command at a later time.

RESET Command

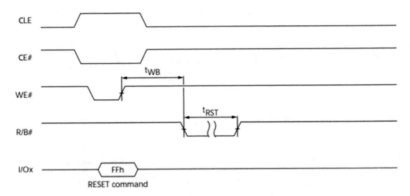

Figure 6-4. *RESET command timing diagram*

READ ID Operation

The READ ID (90h) command requires one dummy address cycle (00h), but it does not require a second command cycle. After the command and dummy addresses are issued, the ID data can be read out by keeping CLE and ALE LOW and toggling the RE# signal for each byte of ID. READ ID response depends on the manufacturer specifications, which typically include Manufacturer ID, Device ID, Cell Type, page size, etc.

READ ID Command

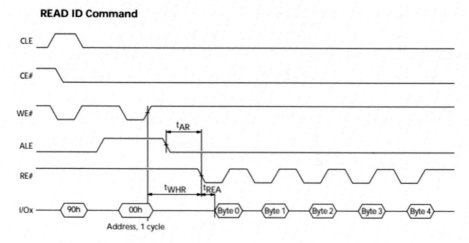

Figure 6-5. *READ ID timing diagram*

READ STATUS Operation

READ STATUS (70h) is the second command that can be issued while the
NAND flash device is busy. This command does not require an address
or second command cycle. The status of the NAND flash device can be
monitored by issuing the RE# clock signal following the READ STATUS
command. If the READ STATUS command is used to monitor the ready
state of the device, the command should be issued only one time, and the
status can be re-read by reissuing the RE# clock. Alternatively, the RE#
signal can be kept LOW, waiting to receive the appropriate status bit before
proceeding. READ STATUS also reports the status of the write-protect signal,
and the pass/fail status of previous PROGRAM or ERASE operations. It is
mandatory that the pass status be attained on PROGRAM or ERASE operations
to ensure proper data integrity.

READ STATUS Response

Table 6-4. *READ STATUS Response Table*

SR Bit	PROGRAM PAGE	PROGRAM PAGE CACHE MODE	PAGE READ	PAGE READ CACHE MODE	BLOCK ERASE	Definition
0	Pass/fail	Pass/fail (N)	–	–	Pass/fail	0 = Successful PROGRAM/ERASE 1 = Error in PROGRAM/ERASE
1	–	Pass/fail (N-1)	–	–	–	0 = Successful PROGRAM/ERASE 1 = Error in PROGRAM/ERASE
2	–	–	–	–	–	0
3	–	–	–	–	–	0
4	–	–	–	–	–	0
5	Ready/busy	Ready/busy[1]	Ready/busy	Ready/busy[1]	Ready/busy	0=Busy 1=Ready
6	Ready/busy	Ready/busy	Ready/busycache[2]	Ready/busy	Ready/busycache[2]	0=Busy 1=Ready
7	Write protect	Write protect	Write protect	Write protect	Write protect	0 = Protected1 = Not protected
[15:8]	–	–	–	–	–	0

Notes: 1. Status register bit 5 is 0 during the actual programming operation. If cache mode is used, this bit will be 1 when all internal operations are complete.

2. Status register bit 6 is 1 when the cache is ready to accept new data. R/B# follows bit 6.

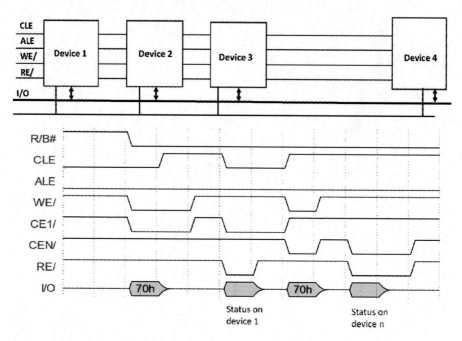

Figure 6-6. *READ STATUS timings application example*

Note   If the Ready/Busy pin signals of multiple devices are common
wired as shown in Figure 6-6, the READ STATUS function can be
used to determine the status of each individually selected device.

ERASE Operation

The BLOCK ERASE (60h) operation erases an entire block. To issue a
BLOCK ERASE operation, use the WE# signal to clock in the ERASE (60h)
command with CLE asserted. Next, clock in three address cycles, keeping

ALE asserted for each byte of address. (These three address cycles are the most significant address cycles and include the block address and the page address.) The page address portion (the six low-order bits of the third address cycle) is ignored, and only the block address portion of the three most significant bytes is used. After the address is inputted completely, issue the second command (command cycle 2) of D0h, which is clocked in with WE# while CLE is being asserted. This confirms the ERASE operation, and the device goes busy for approximately 5us. When the device completes this operation, it is ready for another command. The READ STATUS command can be issued at any time, even when the device is busy during the ERASE operation. The microprocessor or controller can monitor the device via the READ STATUS command.

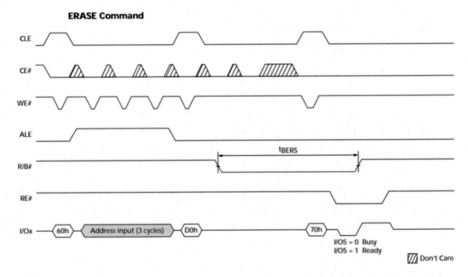

Figure 6-7. *Timing diagram for ERASE BLOCK operation*

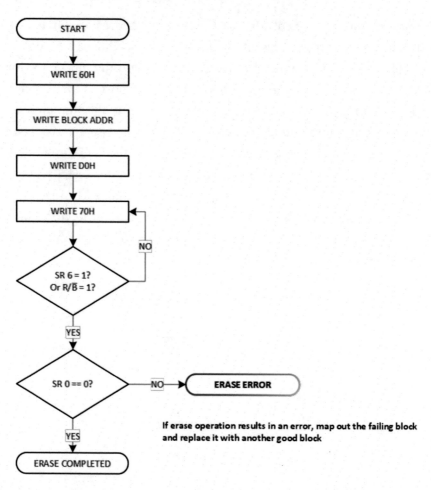

Figure 6-8. *Flow diagram for ERASE BLOCK operation*

PROGRAM Operations

PROGRAM operations can only program bits to 0 and assume that the user
started with a previously erased block. If the user does not want to program
a bit (or group of bits), the bits can be kept in the erased state by setting
that particular bit/group to 1. When the PROGRAM PAGE (80h) command
is received, the input register is reset (internally) to all 1s. This supports

inputting only bytes of data that are to be programmed with 0 bits. The PROGRAM operation starts with the 80h command (with CLE asserted). Next, de-assert CLE and assert ALE to input the full five address cycles. After the command and address are inputted, data is inputted to the register. When all the data has been inputted, the 10h command is issued to confirm the previous command and start the programming operation. It is mandatory that the user read the status and check for successful operation. If the operation is not successful, the block should be logged as a bad block and not be used in the future. All data should be moved to a good block.

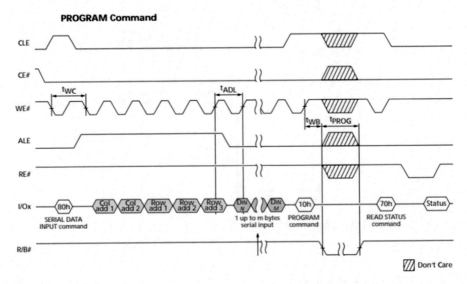

Figure 6-9. *Timing diagram for program operation*

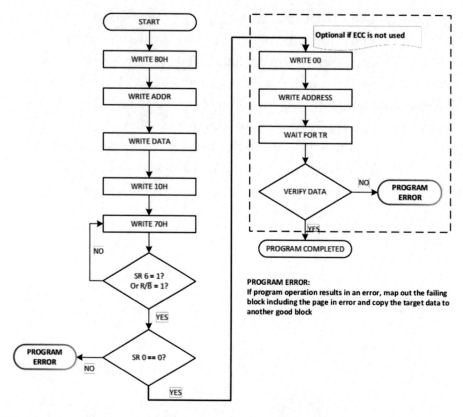

Figure 6-10. *Flow diagram for PROGRAM operation*

READ Operation

A READ operation starts with the 00h command, followed by five address cycles, then the 30h command to confirm the command sequence. After the READ transfer time (tR) has elapsed, the data is loaded into the register and ready for outputting. Asserting RE# enables the NAND flash device to output the first byte of data corresponding to the column address specified. Subsequent RE# transitions output data from successive column locations. When the RE# signal is HIGH (not asserted), the IO lines are tri-stated. Reading past the end of the device results in invalid data.

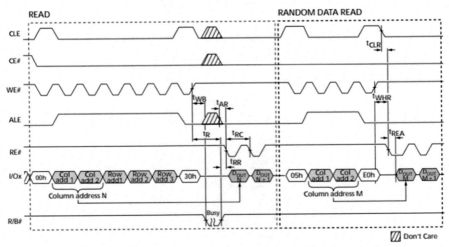

Figure 6-11. *Timing diagram for READ with random data out operation*

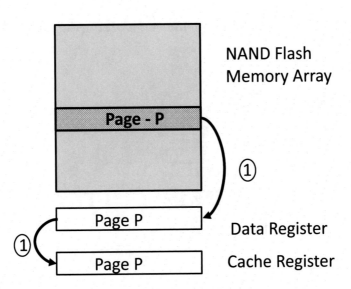

Figure 6-12. *NAND flash array internal working during read operation*

RANDOM DATA READ Operation

The user can directly access random data by issuing the 05h command, two address cycles, and an E0h confirmation cycle. When the page has been read from the array, this command provides rapid access to the data.

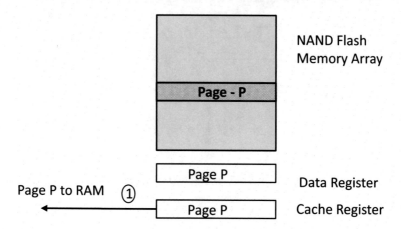

Figure 6-13. *NAND flash array internal working during RANDOM READ DATA out*

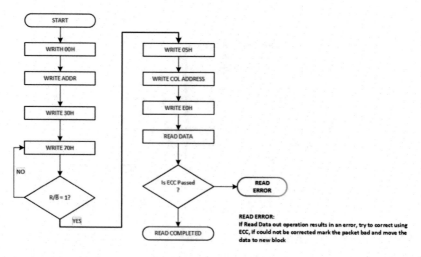

Figure 6-14. *Flow diagram for READ operation with RANDOM DATA out operation*

Typical NAND Packet Structure

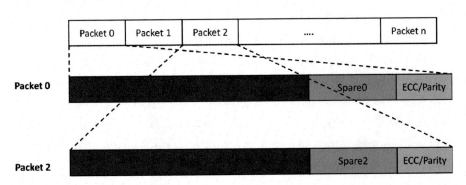

Figure 6-15. *NAND flash internal packet structure*

NAND flash memory utilizes a structured data format known as the NAND PACKET, which comprises both the data area and the spare area. The spare area can be employed to store essential firmware-related information and an error-correcting code (ECC) used for error-correction purposes. In this structure, for example, the data area consists of 512 bytes, and it is accompanied by a 16-byte spare area, creating a total of 528 bytes for the combined areas.

To ensure data integrity, ECC is a critical component in NAND flash. The example NAND flash memory we are considering here includes a 64-byte spare area for each page, with 16 bytes per 512-byte sector. Within this spare area, the ECC can be stored along with other software information, like wear-leveling or logical-to-physical block-mapping details. ECC can be implemented either in hardware or software, with hardware-based implementation offering better performance.

During a programming operation, the ECC unit calculates the ECC based on the data stored in the sector, and the code is then written to the corresponding spare area. When reading out the data, the ECC is also retrieved, and the reverse operation is applied to verify the correctness of the data. The ECC algorithm is capable of correcting data errors, and the level of correction depends on the strength of the algorithm used. This inclusion of ECC, whether in hardware or software, ensures a robust solution at the system level.

For error correction, different ECCs are available, each offering varying levels of correction capability. Simple Hamming codes are the easiest to implement in hardware, but they can only correct single-bit errors. Reed-Solomon codes, however, provide more robust error-correction capabilities and are commonly used in many NAND flash controllers in the market. Additionally, BCH codes are gaining popularity due to their improved efficiency over Reed-Solomon codes.

PAGE READ CACHE MODE Operation

As we have seen before, the NAND flash device actually has two registers: a data register and a cache register. The attributes of these two registers play an important role in the various NAND flash caching modes. The PAGE READ CACHE MODE command enables the user to pipeline the next sequential access from the array while outputting the previously accessed data. This double-buffered technique makes it possible to hide the READ transfer time (tR). Data is initially transferred from the NAND flash array to the data register. If the cache register is available (not busy), the data is quickly moved from the data register to the cache register. After the data has been transferred to the cache register, the data register is available and can start to load the next sequential page from the NAND flash array. Using the PAGE READ CACHE MODE command delivers a performance improvement over a traditional PAGE READ command on an 8-bit input/ output (IO) device. PAGE READ CACHE MODE can be especially useful during system boot-up, when large amounts of data are typically read from the NAND flash device and start-up time is critical.

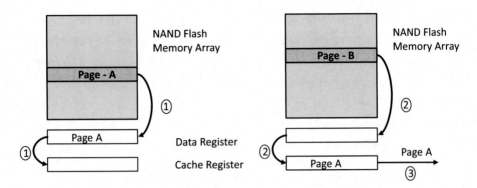

Figure 6-16. *NAND flash array internal working during cache read operation*

READ PAGE/READ PAGE CACHE SEQUENTIAL Comparison

PAGE READ Example

| 00h | Address cycles 1–5 | 30h | tRead | | 00h | Address cycles 1–5 | 30h | tRead | |

Data of Page 0   Data of Page 1

PAGE READ CACHE SEQUENTIAL Example

| 00h | Address cycles 1–5 | 30h | tRead | 31h | 3 µs | | 31h | 3 µs | |

Data of Page 0   Data of Page 1

■ Read busy time   ■ Cache busy time   □ Commands   Address   Data

Figure 6-17. *NAND page read and NAND page cache read timing diagram comparison*

PROGRAM PAGE CACHE Operation

PROGRAM PAGE CACHE MODE provides a performance improvement over normal PROGRAM PAGE operations. PROGRAM PAGE CACHE MODE is a double-buffered technique that enables the controller to input data directly to the cache register and uses the data register as a holding area to supply data for programming the array. This frees the cache register so that the next sequential page operation can be loaded in parallel. In many applications, the programming time (tPROG) can be completely hidden. As with the PAGE READ CACHE MODE command, the data register is used to maintain the data throughput during the entire programming cycle. This frees the cache register to receive the next page of data from the controller.

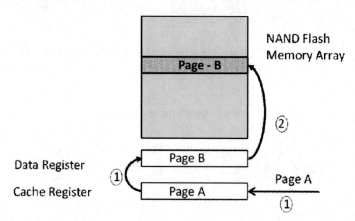

Figure 6-18. *NAND flash array internal working during cache program operation*

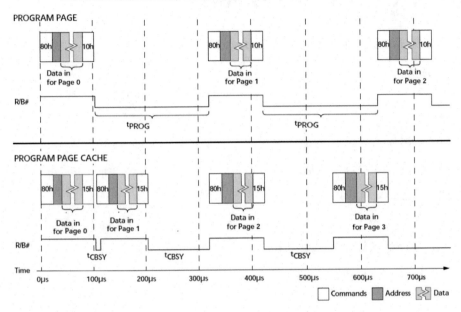

Figure 6-19. *NAND page program and NAND page cache program timing diagram comparison*

Advanced Command Sets

Table 6-5. *NAND Advanced Command Sets*

Command	Command Cycle Set- 1	Number of Address Cycles Set-1	Command Cycle Set-2	Number of Address Cycles Set-2
MULTI PLANE READ	00h – 32h	5	00h – 30h	5
READ PAGE CACHE SEQUENTIAL	00h – 32h	–	00h – 31h	5
RANDOM DATA READ OUTPUT	05h	5	E0h	-
MULTI PLANE PROGRAM PAGE	80h – 11h	5	80h – 10h	5
MULTI PLANE PROGRAM PAGE CACHE	80h – 11h	5	80h – 1Ah	5
ERASE BLOCK	60h	3	D0h	-

As NAND flash technology continues to evolve, manufacturers have introduced extended command sets to enhance the performance and efficiency of these memory devices. These extended commands provide additional capabilities beyond the standard commands traditionally used with NAND flash. Understanding and utilizing these extended commands can greatly improve the overall performance and reliability of the storage device.

Extended NAND commands enable more efficient data transfer and management, making them particularly valuable in scenarios where speed and responsiveness are crucial, which is necessary even in an SD card. These commands allow simultaneous reading or writing from multiple planes within the NAND flash, significantly improving data access rates.

By leveraging these capabilities, developers can optimize read and write operations, making their device more responsive and efficient.

One of the key features of extended NAND commands is their ability to support multi-plane operations. With multi-plane reads, multiple data planes can be accessed simultaneously, reducing latency and boosting read performance. Similarly, multi-plane writes allow data to be programmed into multiple planes concurrently, speeding up the writing process and enhancing overall write efficiency.

Another advantage of extended NAND commands is their support for cache operations. Multi-plane cache reads and writes (double-buffered technique) makes it possible to hide the read transfer tREAD /program time: tPROG, further improving system performance. This double-buffered technique makes it possible to hide the READ transfer time (tR). Data is initially transferred from the NAND flash array to the data register for both the planes simultaneously. If the cache register is available (not busy), the data is quickly moved from the data register to the cache register in both planes.

Address Input Restrictions for Multi-Plane Operations

Multi-plane capability can significantly enhance data transfer rates and improve overall system performance. However, when utilizing multi-plane operations, there are specific address input restrictions that must be followed to enable this functionality correctly, as follows:

- **Sequential Addressing:** When performing multi-plane operations, the NAND flash memory requires sequential addressing of pages within each plane. This means that the pages accessed in a multi-plane operation should be in consecutive order within their respective planes. Sequential addressing ensures efficient data retrieval and programming, as the NAND flash device can optimize the internal read and write operations for consecutive page access instances.

- **Identical Page Select Command:** For each plane involved in a multi-plane operation, the `Page Select` command must be identical. This command specifies the page address within the block and helps the NAND flash device identify the specific pages that need to be accessed in the multi-plane operation. By using the same `Page Select` command for all planes, the NAND flash memory can effectively synchronize the read or write operations across different planes.

- **Address Set Commands:** The address input for multi-plane operations requires a specific sequence of address set commands. These commands are responsible for loading the address information into the NAND flash memory before the multi-plane read or write operation can be initiated. The first and second sets of commands must be used to set the page address and block address, respectively. Careful adherence to this sequence ensures that the NAND flash device correctly interprets the addresses and performs the intended multi-plane operation.

- **Boundary Limitations:** Multi-plane operations must be confined within a block of each plane. Crossing the boundaries of different planes during a multi-plane operation is not supported. Thus, all the pages involved in a multi-plane operation should belong to the same block within their respective planes. This limitation ensures that the multi-plane operations are effectively contained within the boundaries of each block, avoiding any data conflicts or data corruption that might occur when operating across block boundaries.

Multi-plane Read

The Multi-Plane Read operation is an extension of the standard Page Read operation. It allows reading data from multiple pages simultaneously, which enhances read performance. After issuing the command cycle set-1 commands, the device quickly returns to the ready state, and data from the selected pages are transferred to cache registers. The multi-plane addresses are set through specific commands. Once the data is loaded into the cache registers, it can be read out using the MULTI PLANE RANDOM DATA OUTPUT command. The Page Select command should be the same between planes in the repeatable sequence. This enables efficient and rapid access to data from multiple pages within the NAND flash memory.

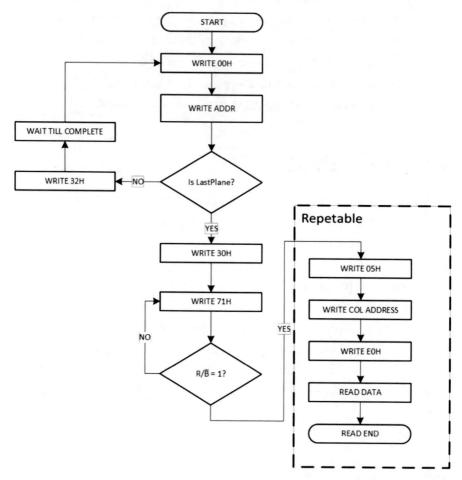

Figure 6-20. *Flow diagram for multi-plane read with random data out operation*

MULTI- PLANE RANDOM CACHE READ Operation

The Multi Plane Random Cache Read function allows reading data from multiple pages into the cache registers ahead of the command 31h. This operation is beneficial as it allows for faster access to data since the selected pages are loaded into the page register while the host reads data from the cache register. This process enables a quick return to the ready state (R/B HIGH) unless the previous data is still being loaded. The multi-plane addresses are set through specific commands, and the activated planes for the first Multi Plane Random Cache Read are retained for subsequent address sequences until the Multi Plane Random Cache operation is completed with command 3Fh. It's important to use identical Page Select commands between planes within the repeatable sequence. This mechanism optimizes data retrieval and improves overall read performance from multiple pages within the NAND flash memory.

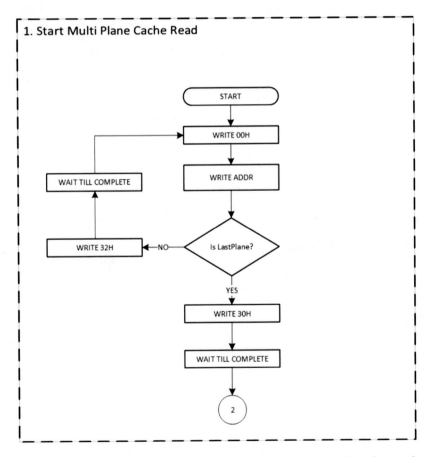

Figure 6-21. *Flow diagram for multi-plane cache read with random data out operation*

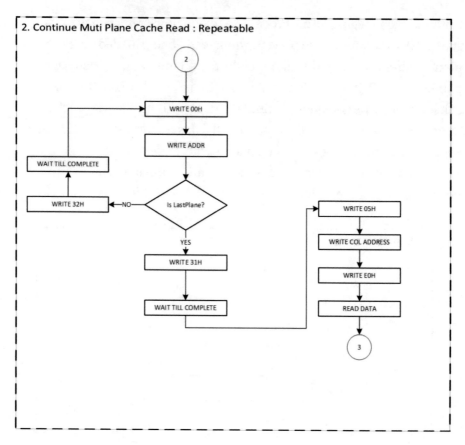

Figure 6-21. *(continued)*

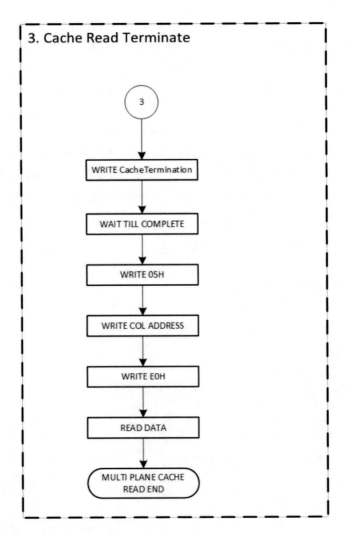

Figure 6-21. *(continued)*

Multi Plane Program Operation

The Multi Plane Full Sequence Program function expands the effective programmable page size by using multiple pages. The host can load data for another page using command 11h as the second command. After issuing the 11h command, the R/B signal returns HIGH (ready state) in a short period since it is not an actual programming operation. When loading data for the last page, the command 80h is used before loading data, and command 1Ah/10h is issued after data loading as the second command. After the command 10h, all the data loaded into each page starts to be programmed simultaneously into the flash array. It's important to ensure that the multi-plane addresses are correctly set through the first and second sets of commands. This feature enables an efficient and streamlined process for programming data across multiple pages, effectively extending the programmable page size in the NAND flash memory.

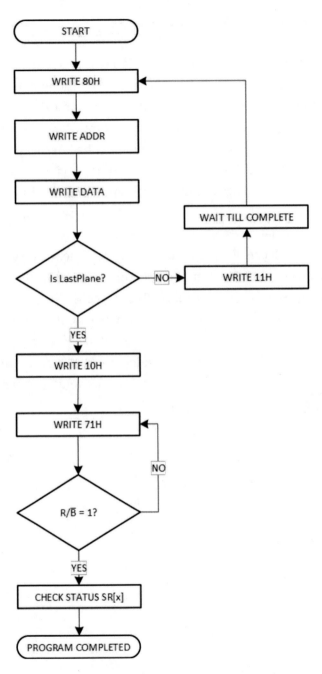

Figure 6-22. *Flow diagram for multi-plane program operation*

Multi Plane Cache Program Operation

The Multi Plane Cache Full Sequence Program is an enhanced version of the Cache Full Sequence Program. In this operation, multiple pages are loaded for programming, and then command 15h is issued. After that command, R/B returns HIGH once the transfer of data from the cache register to the page register is completed. The internal program operation begins after R/B returns, while other pages can still be loaded by the host. At the final page loading for the entire Multi Plane Cache Program, command 10h is needed to complete the operation, and R/B stays busy for a specific period known as tPROG. It's essential to note that the Multi Plane Cache Program should only be done within a block of each plane and should not extend beyond the boundary of the plane. The activated planes for the first Multi Plane Cache Full Sequence Program will be used in the next address sequence until the entire Multi Plane Cache Full Sequence Program is completed by command 10h. This feature allows efficient and coordinated programming of multiple pages in the NAND flash memory, enhancing the overall performance and functionality of the device.

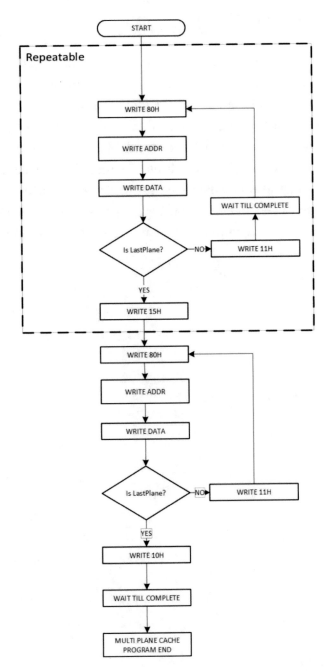

Figure 6-23. *Flow diagram for multi-plane cache program operation*

Multi Block Erase Operation

`Multi Block Erase` provides the option to erase multiple blocks, with each block belonging to a different plane, all at the same time. However, it's essential to note that the same plane address should not be set twice within a set of address settings for the `Multi Block Erase` operation. This restriction ensures that blocks from each plane are only erased once and prevents any unintended or duplicate erasures, thereby maintaining data integrity and preventing data loss. By utilizing `Multi Block Erase`, developers can efficiently manage and erase multiple blocks, optimizing the overall performance and management of the NAND flash memory device.

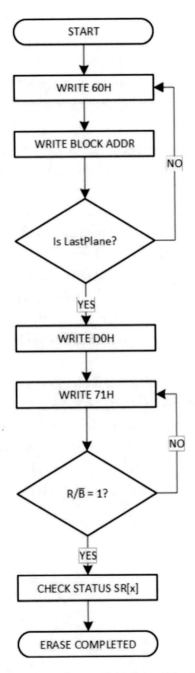

Figure 6-24. *Flow diagram for multi-plane block erase operation*

Summary

In conclusion, this chapter provided a brief overview of the fundamental concepts and principles behind interfacing with NAND flash memory. We began by introducing hardware-interfacing aspects, and also explored the pin configurations, signal descriptions, and timing diagrams essential for proper communication between the NAND flash memory and the CPU/processor. We explored the multi-plane operation, a powerful feature of 3D vertical NAND that allows simultaneous access to multiple pages in different planes. Understanding the address input restrictions and command sequences for multi-plane operations is essential for maximizing the benefits of this technology.

Moreover, we looked into the NAND flash interface standards, such as ONFI (Open NAND Flash Interface) specification and Toggle Mode DDR NAND interface. Standardization plays a crucial role in ensuring compatibility, interoperability, and ease of integration in various applications.

A robust understanding of NAND flash memory interfacing is vital for engineers and developers working on embedded systems, solid-state drives, and various other applications. By grasping the concepts covered in this chapter, they can design efficient, optimized, and reliable NAND flash-based solutions that cater to a wide range of industries and meet the diverse needs of modern computing and data storage.

CHAPTER 7

Common SSD Firmware Features

In this chapter, we will discuss the common solid-state drive (SSD) firmware features. We will start by discussing the mapping table, which is used to store the mapping between logical block addresses (LBAs) and physical block addresses (PBAs). We will then discuss bad block management, which is used to identify and manage bad blocks on the drive. We will also discuss wear leveling, which is used to distribute writes evenly across the drive to extend its lifespan. Garbage collection is another important feature that is used to reclaim unused space on the drive. We will also discuss data retention, error handling, power-loss protection, and unexpected shutdown support.

Wear leveling is a technique used by SSD firmware to distribute writes across the drive in an efficient manner, with the goal of extending the lifespan of the drive. Because an SSD has a limited number of program/erase cycles before the memory cells begin to degrade, it is important to ensure that the cells are written to an equal number of times. Wear-leveling algorithms in SSD firmware select the best blocks (lower P/E cycle count) to erase and to distribute writes to in a way that maximizes the number of available blocks for writing.

Static wear leveling helps to prevent the problem of non-uniform usage of blocks in a block pool by identifying the cold data on the drive and relocating it to a block with a high program/erase count. In some

© Gopi Kuppan Thirumalai 2023
G. Kuppan Thirumalai, *A Beginner's Guide to SSD Firmware*,
https://doi.org/10.1007/978-1-4842-9888-6_7

cases, a block may hold "cold" data that is not overwritten by the host for a long time, causing that block to not be freed for erasure and reuse. This can lead to uneven distribution of program/erase (P/E) cycles among the blocks, with some blocks reaching their end of life sooner than others. The wear-leveling scheme identifies such "cold" blocks and moves their data to a "hot" block, allowing the cold block to be erased and used again. This helps to distribute P/E cycles evenly among all blocks in the pool, prolonging the overall lifespan of the block pool.

Garbage collection is a related process that is used to reclaim space on an SSD that has been marked as no longer in use. This can involve consolidating data from multiple blocks into a single block and then erasing the original blocks.

The main objective of garbage collection is to free up available blocks in a system by moving valid data from a source block with less-valid data to a new block. This allows the space in the source block to be reclaimed and used again. One approach to choosing which block to free up is for the firmware to maintain a count of the valid data in each block and select the block with the least amount of valid data for garbage collection.

However, the writes involved in compaction, which is the process of moving valid data from the source block to a new block, are not initiated by the host. This results in a phenomenon known as write amplification, where the SSD is written more than the amount of data originally received from the host. Write amplification increases the number of program/ erase (P/E) cycles on the SSD, which can impact the host write speed and shorten the lifespan of the SSD. Therefore, it is important to minimize the need for compaction operations and only perform them when necessary.

In addition to freeing up space in the source block, another objective of garbage collection is to move data from a block that is experiencing errors to a healthy block. This helps to avoid data loss due to errors in the NAND flash memory, which can occur over time as the number of P/E cycles increases. By moving the data from a bad block to a good block, you ensure the data can still be accessed by the host without error.

Significance of Garbage Collection in SSDs

Fragmentation occurs as a result of data updates and deletions, leading to scattered data blocks across the NAND flash memory. Garbage collection helps consolidate these blocks, reducing the need for scattered reads and writes and improving performance. This is because when the data is compacted together, they are more likely to be located in contiguous memory blocks. This makes it easier for the flash controller to access the data, which can lead to improved performance.

Types of Garbage Collection Strategies

Full Garbage Collection

Full garbage collection, also known as complete garbage collection, involves the relocation and consolidation of all valid data blocks within the NAND flash memory. Its objective is to eliminate fragmentation entirely by moving data blocks to contiguous regions. This type of garbage collection is typically performed during idle or low-activity periods when the SSD has sufficient available resources to carry out the extensive relocation process.

Full garbage collection offers the advantage of achieving optimal storage utilization and minimizing write amplification. By consolidating data blocks, it reduces the need for scattered read and write operations, resulting in improved overall performance. However, full garbage collection can be time consuming and resource intensive, making it less suitable for an application/workload with frequent write operations.

Partial Garbage Collection

Partial garbage collection involves the relocation and consolidation of only a subset of valid data blocks within the NAND flash memory. Unlike full garbage collection, partial garbage collection targets specific areas or segments of the SSD that exhibit higher fragmentation or higher invalid block density.

Partial garbage collection strikes a balance between the benefits of full garbage collection and the resources required to perform the operation. It helps reduce write amplification and improves performance in specific areas prone to fragmentation. By selectively addressing regions with higher fragmentation, partial garbage collection provides a more efficient approach for optimizing storage utilization and enhancing overall SSD performance.

Dynamic Garbage Collection

Dynamic garbage collection combines elements of both full and partial garbage collection strategies. It dynamically determines the level of garbage collection required based on real-time workload and system conditions. The decision to perform either full or partial garbage collection is made by the SSD firmware based on factors such as the level of fragmentation, the available resources, and the workload intensity.

Dynamic garbage collection offers the flexibility to adapt garbage-collection operations to the specific needs of the SSD. It optimizes performance by selectively targeting heavily fragmented areas while minimizing the impact on overall system resources. By dynamically adjusting the garbage-collection approach, SSDs can strike a balance between performance optimization and resource utilization, ensuring efficient data management in varying workload scenarios.

Error-Triggered Garbage Collection

Error-triggered garbage collection is a specialized type of garbage collection that is initiated in response to program errors, read errors, or erase errors encountered during SSD operation. These errors can include issues such as uncorrectable bit errors, unresponsive blocks, program failure, or failed erase operations. When such errors occur, the SSD firmware triggers a dedicated garbage-collection process to relocate data from the problematic blocks, mark the blocks as invalid, and reclaim them for future use.

Error-triggered garbage collection aims to mitigate the impact of errors on SSD performance and data integrity. By promptly identifying and handling faulty blocks, it helps to maintain the overall health and reliability of the SSD. This type of garbage collection ensures that erroneous blocks are not used for data storage, minimizing the chances of data corruption or loss.

Engineers need to carefully consider the types of garbage-collection strategies based on the specific SSD characteristics, workload patterns, and performance requirements of their systems. The choice of full, partial, or dynamic garbage collection can have a significant impact on the efficiency, performance, and longevity of the SSD. Understanding these strategies empowers engineers to design and implement effective garbage-collection algorithms tailored to the unique needs of their applications and environments.

Garbage Collection Read Process

The garbage collection read process is a critical step within the garbage-collection mechanism of an SSD. During garbage collection, valid data is relocated and consolidated to optimize storage efficiency. In this chapter, we will explore the garbage collection read process in detail, focusing on retrieving valid data, handling incomplete or interrupted reads, and the role of address translation during compaction reads.

Retrieving Valid Data during Compaction

During the garbage-collection process, the SSD firmware needs to retrieve valid data from the blocks that are being compacted. This involves reading the contents of the valid data blocks that will be relocated. The firmware accesses the NAND flash memory to retrieve the stored data, which can include file contents, application data, or any other user data.

To retrieve the valid data, the firmware utilizes the mapping table, which contains the mapping between logical block addresses (LBAs) and their corresponding physical block addresses (PBAs). The mapping table allows the firmware to accurately locate the physical location of the data within the NAND flash memory. By referencing the mapping table, the firmware can identify the specific valid data blocks that need to be read during the compaction process.

Once the garbage collection is completed, the firmware must ensure that the valid data is still accessible. This is done by maintaining a mapping of the old and new locations of data. When a read request is received, the firmware first checks the mapping to see if the data has been compacted. If it has, the firmware then reads the data from the new location.

Handling Incomplete or Interrupted Reads

It is possible for a read request to be interrupted before it is completed. This can happen if the SSD is powered off or if the firmware encounters an error. When this happens, the firmware must resume the read request from the point at which it was interrupted to restart the relocation process gracefully. To ensure data integrity and maintain the consistency of the compaction process, the SSD firmware employs error-handling and error-correction mechanisms. These mechanisms involve implementing error-detection codes, such as cyclic redundancy checks (CRC), and error-correction codes, such as Reed-Solomon codes.

If an incomplete or interrupted read occurs, the firmware can use the error-detection and -correction codes to identify and rectify any potential errors in the read data. By applying these error-correction techniques, the firmware can recover the missing or corrupted data and ensure the successful completion of the compaction process.

Address Translation during Compaction Reads

Address translation plays a crucial role during the compaction read process. The firmware utilizes the address translation mechanisms to convert the logical block addresses (LBAs) into their corresponding physical block addresses (PBAs) when retrieving valid data.

The address translation process involves accessing the mapping table, which stores the LBAs and their corresponding PBAs. By looking up the mapping table, the firmware can obtain the accurate physical location of the data within the NAND flash memory. This translation allows the firmware to read the correct data blocks during the compaction process and maintain the integrity of the data.

The mapping table is a key aspect of SSD operations and is essential for efficient data retrieval and management. The firmware's ability to accurately translate LBAs into PBAs ensures that valid data is correctly accessed during the compaction read process.

Once the garbage collection is completed, the mapping table must be updated to reflect the new location of data. This is done by the firmware during the compaction process. When a read request is received, the firmware first checks the mapping table to see if the address has been updated. If it has, the firmware then uses the new address to read the data.

By understanding the intricacies of the compaction read process, designers and engineers can develop effective garbage-collection algorithms and optimize the performance of SSDs. Considerations such as data retrieval, error handling, and address translation contribute to the overall reliability and efficiency of the compaction read process in SSD firmware.

Here are some additional details about the compaction read process:

- The compaction read process is a complex operation that requires careful coordination between the firmware and the hardware.

- The firmware should maintain a mapping of the old and new locations of data.

- The firmware must handle incomplete or interrupted reads gracefully.

- The firmware must update the mapping table to reflect the new location of data.

Writing Data during Compaction

During the garbage-collection process, when valid data blocks are relocated and consolidated the SSD firmware must write the data to the new blocks and free up the source blocks. This process ensures that the data remains accessible and retrievable after compaction.

The firmware retrieves the valid data from the source blocks and writes it to the target blocks. The actual data transfer occurs by programming the NAND flash memory cells with the valid data from source blocks. The firmware ensures that the data is accurately written to the target blocks, preserving the integrity of the information.

Address Mapping and Updating

Address mapping and updating play a crucial role in the compaction write process. As the valid data is moved to new blocks, the firmware must update the corresponding address mappings in the mapping table. This update ensures that the logical block addresses (LBAs) are correctly associated with the new physical block addresses (PBAs).

The firmware modifies the mapping table entries to reflect the new mappings between LBAs and PBAs. By updating the mapping table, the firmware maintains an accurate translation between LBAs requested by the host system and the physical location of the data within the NAND flash memory.

Managing Block Erasure and Wear-Leveling

As part of the compaction write process, the SSD firmware must manage block erasure and consider wear leveling while allocating new blocks. When data is relocated to new blocks, the source blocks become invalid and are eligible for erasure to reclaim them for future use.

The firmware schedules the erasure of the invalidated blocks, typically during idle periods or when there is sufficient available time for the operation. By erasing these blocks, the firmware ensures that they are ready to be used for new data storage, optimizing the efficiency of the NAND flash memory.

Additionally, wear-leveling mechanisms come into play during the compaction write process; i.e., when a new target block is chosen. The firmware evenly distributes write operations across the blocks, preventing specific blocks from experiencing excessive wear. This approach extends the overall lifespan and reliability of the SSD by maintaining balanced usage of the NAND flash memory.

Effective management of block erasure and wear leveling is crucial for maintaining the performance and longevity of an SSD. Properly handling these aspects during the compaction write process ensures efficient data relocation, optimal storage utilization, and prolonged SSD lifespan.

By understanding the intricacies of the compaction write process, designers and engineers can develop robust garbage-collection algorithms and optimize the performance of SSDs. The accurate writing of data, address mapping and updating, and effective block erasure and wear-leveling management contribute to the overall reliability and efficiency of the compaction write process in SSD firmware.

Handling Unexpected Power-Off Conditions in Garbage Collection

Handling unexpected power-off conditions is a critical aspect of the garbage-collection mechanism in an SSD. Power-loss events can occur unexpectedly and pose a risk to data consistency and system stability. A design should be considered for handling unexpected power-off conditions in garbage collection, including ensuring data consistency during power loss, write journaling and recovery mechanisms, and managing incomplete compaction operations.

Ensuring Data Consistency during Power Loss

During the garbage-collection process, an unexpected power loss can interrupt ongoing compaction operations (either read from source blocks or while writing to destination block, or while updating the mapping table), potentially leading to data inconsistencies. It is crucial to ensure data consistency, even in the face of power failures.

To do so, the SSD firmware employs various mechanisms, including transactional updates and atomic operations. These mechanisms ensure that compaction operations are performed in a consistent and atomic manner. Atomic operations ensure that either all or none of the updates related to compaction are applied, preventing partial or inconsistent modifications.

Furthermore, the firmware may employ techniques such as write buffering or power-loss protection capacitors. Write buffering temporarily stores data in volatile memory before it is permanently written to the NAND flash memory. Power-loss protection capacitors provide enough energy to complete ongoing write operations and safely flush buffered data in the event of a sudden power loss.

By implementing these techniques, the firmware minimizes the risk of data corruption or loss during unexpected power-off conditions, maintaining data consistency in the face of power failures.

Write Journaling and Recovery Mechanisms

Write journaling is a common technique used to handle unexpected power-off conditions in garbage collection. It involves keeping a log or journal of write operations during the compaction process. The write journal captures the modifications made to the mapping table and data blocks.

In the event of an unexpected power loss, the firmware can consult the write journal upon system restart. By replaying the recorded write operations, the firmware can recover the system to a consistent state and ensure the integrity of the compaction process.

Recovery mechanisms are employed to resume or recover incomplete compaction operations after a power loss. These mechanisms involve identifying the point of interruption and resuming or reperforming the necessary compaction steps from that point onward. The recovery process ensures that the SSD can continue the garbage collection process without compromising data integrity or system stability.

Managing Incomplete Compaction Operations

In the event of a power loss or system interruption during compaction, the SSD firmware must handle incomplete operations to maintain the integrity of the garbage-collection process.

The firmware employs techniques such as rollback or forward recovery to manage incomplete compaction operations. Rollback involves undoing or reverting the partially completed operations to return the system to a consistent state. Forward recovery, meanwhile, involves resuming or completing the remaining operations from the point of interruption.

During recovery, the firmware may perform additional checks, such as verifying the integrity of the data or looking for any inconsistencies caused by the interruption. These checks help ensure that the recovered compaction process does not introduce data errors or inconsistencies.

By effectively managing incomplete compaction operations, the firmware minimizes the impact of power-loss events and ensures that the garbage-collection process can be resumed or recovered without data corruption or loss.

Proper handling of unexpected power-off conditions in garbage collection is crucial for maintaining data consistency, system stability, and the overall reliability of an SSD. Ensuring data consistency during power loss, implementing write journaling and recovery mechanisms, and managing incomplete compaction operations contribute to the robustness and effectiveness of the garbage-collection process.

Performance Considerations in Garbage Collection

Performance must be considered when designing and implementing garbage-collection algorithms in SSD firmware. In this section, we will explore the various performance considerations associated with garbage collection. We will discuss the impact of compaction on SSD performance, the concept of write amplification, and strategies to minimize performance degradation.

Impact of Compaction on SSD Performance

The compaction process in garbage collection can have an impact on the performance of an SSD. As valid data is relocated and consolidated, the following factors come into play:

- **Read Performance:** During compaction, the firmware needs to read valid data from the source blocks and write it to the target blocks. The time required for these read operations can impact overall read performance. If the compaction process involves a significant amount of data movement, it can lead to increased read latencies.

- **Write Performance:** The write performance of an SSD can be affected during compaction due to the extensive write operations involved. Writing valid data to new blocks and updating the mapping table can increase the write workload on the NAND flash memory, potentially resulting in longer write latencies.

- **Overhead:** Garbage collection introduces additional overhead in terms of CPU utilization and memory resources. The firmware needs to manage various data structures, perform address translation, and handle error correction, all of which require computational resources.

- To minimize the impact of compaction on SSD performance, firmware designers must optimize garbage-collection algorithms, utilize efficient data management techniques, and leverage SSD-specific optimizations.

Write Amplification and Its Effects

Write amplification is a critical factor that affects SSD performance and longevity. It refers to the ratio between the amount of data written by the host system and the actual amount of data programmed into the NAND flash memory.

During the compaction process, write amplification can occur due to several factors, including the following:

- **Data Relocation:** When valid data is moved from source blocks to target blocks, additional data movement and rewriting may be required. This can result in a higher amount of data being written to the NAND flash memory than what was initially written by the host system.

- **Mapping Table Updates:** Updating the mapping table with new address mappings during compaction requires additional write operations to NAND, contributing to write amplification.

Higher write amplification leads to increased wear on the NAND flash memory and reduced overall SSD lifespan. It also impacts write performance and can result in decreased write endurance.

Strategies to Minimize Performance Degradation

To mitigate the performance degradation caused by compaction and write amplification, the following strategies can be employed:

- **Efficient Data Placement:** Optimizing data placement during compaction can minimize the need for scattered read and write operations. By consolidating data and placing it sequentially, read and write performance can be improved.

- **Dynamic Compaction:** Implementing dynamic compaction techniques allows the firmware to adjust the compaction process based on workload patterns. By intelligently managing the compaction workload, the firmware can optimize performance and resource utilization.

- **Advanced Garbage-Collection Algorithms:** Designing and implementing advanced garbage-collection algorithms can help minimize the frequency and impact of compaction operations. These algorithms intelligently identify and prioritize the most fragmented or invalid blocks for compaction, reducing unnecessary data movement.

- **Write Optimization Techniques:** Leveraging write optimization techniques, such as write combining or coalescing, can reduce the number of write operations required during compaction, minimizing write amplification and improving write performance.

By incorporating these strategies, firmware designers can mitigate the performance degradation caused by compaction and write amplification, resulting in improved overall SSD performance, longevity, and user experience.

Balancing Garbage Collection and Host Write Operations

Balancing the workload between garbage collection and host write operations is crucial for maintaining optimal performance and efficiency in SSDs. In this section, we will explore various strategies and techniques to achieve a balance between garbage collection and host write operations, ensuring smooth operation and maximizing the lifespan of the SSD.

Understanding the Workload Characteristics

To effectively balance garbage collection and host write operations, it is essential to understand the workload characteristics of the system. Analyzing the workload patterns, such as write intensity, read-to-write ratio, and data access patterns, provides insight into the optimal distribution of resources between garbage collection and host write operations.

By monitoring and analyzing the workload, firmware designers can make informed decisions on when and how frequently to trigger garbage-collection processes, considering the workload's impact on performance, wear leveling, and overall system stability.

Garbage Collection Prioritization

Garbage collection can be prioritized to ensure a balanced workload. It involves determining the order and scheduling of garbage-collection processes based on various factors, such as block fragmentation, block erasure count, or data invalidation rate.

Critical factors to consider in prioritizing garbage collection include avoiding excessive write amplification, minimizing data migration, and preventing fragmentation. By prioritizing garbage collection based on these factors, firmware designers can prevent performance degradation and optimize the utilization of resources.

Dynamic Resource Allocation

Dynamic resource allocation is a technique that involves dynamically adjusting the allocation of system resources, such as CPU cycles, memory, and IO bandwidth, between garbage collection and host write operations. This technique allows the firmware to adaptively allocate resources based on the current system workload and requirements.

During periods of high host write activity, resources can be allocated to prioritize host write operations, ensuring that application-level performance is not compromised. Conversely, during periods of lower write activity, more resources can be dedicated to garbage collection to minimize the impact of garbage-collection processes on the system's performance.

Over-Provisioning

Over-provisioning is the practice of reserving a portion of the NAND flash memory capacity for garbage-collection and wear-leveling purposes. By allocating a reserved space, typically a percentage of the total SSD capacity, firmware designers can ensure sufficient free blocks are available for garbage collection without impacting the available storage capacity for host write operations.

Over-provisioning helps to mitigate write amplification, reduce data migration frequency, and extend the lifespan of the SSD. Firmware designers can adjust the amount of over-provisioning based on the specific requirements and characteristics of the system.

Adaptive Garbage Collection

Adaptive garbage collection techniques utilize algorithms that dynamically adjust the garbage-collection process based on real-time workload conditions. These algorithms monitor factors such as write patterns, free block availability, and wear leveling to determine the most suitable time and intensity for garbage collection.

By adapting garbage collection operations to the workload, firmware designers can ensure an optimal balance between garbage collection and host write operations. This approach helps prevent excessive performance degradation and ensures efficient resource utilization.

Drawbacks of Garbage Collection and Minimizing Their Impact

Garbage collection presents certain drawbacks that can impact the overall efficiency and lifespan of the SSD. Following are some of the drawbacks of garbage collection and strategies to minimize their impact.

Write Amplification

One of the primary drawbacks of garbage collection is write amplification, which refers to the increased number of write operations performed by the SSD compared to the writes initiated by the host system. Garbage collection involves moving valid data from source blocks to target blocks, which can result in additional writes due to data migrations, metadata updates, and address mapping modifications.

Performance Degradation

Garbage collection can lead to performance degradation, primarily due to increased read and write latencies caused by data movements and additional operations. The extensive read and write operations involved in garbage collection can consume CPU cycles, memory resources, and IO bandwidth, affecting the overall performance of the SSD.

Increased Power Consumption

Garbage collection can result in increased power consumption due to additional read, write, and erase operations. These operations consume energy and contribute to the overall power consumption of the SSD.

Impact on Endurance

Garbage collection can contribute to the wear-out of NAND flash memory cells. Each program-erase cycle affects the lifespan of the memory, and garbage-collection operations involve numerous write and erase operations.

Firmware designers can employ the following strategies to mitigate the drawbacks of garbage collection:

- Optimizing the garbage-collection algorithm to minimize the time and resources required for data movements.

- Utilizing adaptive garbage-collection algorithms that dynamically adjust the intensity and timing of garbage collection based on workload patterns.

- Employing techniques like parallelization to distribute the computational load across multiple cores or processing units.

By minimizing the performance impact of garbage collection, the SSD can maintain optimal responsiveness and throughput. The following are ways to do so:

- Utilize advanced wear-leveling techniques to evenly distribute write operations across the NAND flash memory.

- Employ write optimization strategies such as write combining or coalescing to reduce the number of write operations during garbage collection.

By minimizing write amplification, the impact on the SSD's performance, endurance, and lifespan can be significantly reduced.

Other Concerns
Data Retention

Data retention is another important concept in SSD firmware design. Because an SSD has no moving parts, it is less susceptible to physical damage than is a traditional hard disk drive (HDD). However, SSDs can still lose data for a variety of reasons, including the failure of memory chips or the corruption of data. "Data retention" also refers to the amount of time that data stored on an SSD can be retained and remain readable after the power has been turned off. This is an important consideration when choosing an SSD, as data retention is a key factor in the reliability and long-term performance of the drive.

There are a few different factors that can affect data retention in an SSD, including the type of memory technology used, the design and quality of the drive, and the ambient temperature and humidity conditions in which the drive is stored.

In general, SSDs tend to have longer data retention periods than traditional hard drives, as they do not have moving parts and are less susceptible to physical wear and tear. However, it is important to note that all SSDs will eventually lose their stored data, and the data retention period will vary depending on the specific drive and its usage conditions.

Periodic read is a data retention mechanism used in some SSD firmware to periodically read and verify the data stored on the drive. This process helps to identify and correct any errors that may have occurred during the writing or reading of data, and can improve the overall reliability and data retention of the drive. Periodic reads are typically performed automatically by the drive without the need for user intervention. These mechanisms are usually used in conjunction with other data retention techniques, such as wear-leveling algorithms and error-correcting codes, in order to ensure the maximum possible data retention period for the drive.

Read Disturb

When reading data from NAND flash memory, a phenomenon called **read disturb** can occur, causing neighboring cells in the same memory block to unintentionally change over time. This happens when a cell is read repeatedly without any intervening erase operations. Although the read cell itself may not fail, one of the nearby cells may experience a change during a subsequent read.

To prevent the read disturb issue, the flash controller keeps track of the total number of reads to a specific block since the last erase. Once this count exceeds a predetermined limit, the affected block's data is copied to a new block, then the affected block is erased and added back to the available block pool. After the erase process, the original block is essentially restored to its initial condition.

If the flash controller fails to intervene in a timely manner, a read disturb error may occur. In such cases, if the errors are too numerous to correct using an error-correcting code, data loss could potentially happen.

To ensure data integrity and prevent read disturb–related errors, the flash controller actively manages the number of reads to each block, copying and erasing blocks as necessary. This intervention helps maintain the reliability and long-term performance of the NAND flash memory.

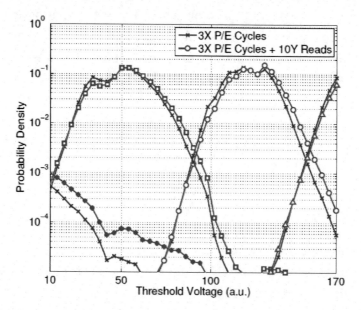

Figure 7-1. *Read disturb probability based on P/E cycle*

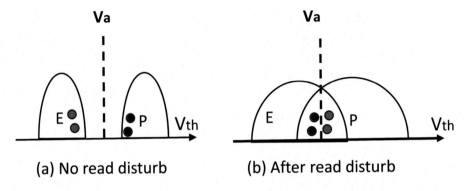

Figure 7-2. *Vth distributions before and after read disturb*

Program Disturbance

Program disturbance is a phenomenon that can occur when an SSD is being written to, in which the process of writing to one page can cause the data on nearby pages to become corrupted. This can be a particular problem in multi-level cell (MLC) SSDs, which store multiple bits of data per memory cell, which can potentially affect the integrity of the data stored on the drive.

To minimize the effects of program disturbance, SSD firmware includes algorithms that perform a read-and-verify operation immediately after writing the physical page data to the drive. This operation involves reading back the data that was just written to the drive and comparing it to the original data to ensure that it was written correctly (ECC check). Depending on the specific scheme implemented in the firmware, this read-and-verify operation may be performed immediately after writing the data, or it may be performed after a delayed interval.

Overall, the use of algorithms to minimize the effects of program disturbance and recover from silent read failure is an important part of the firmware in SSDs and helps to ensure the reliability and data retention of the drive.

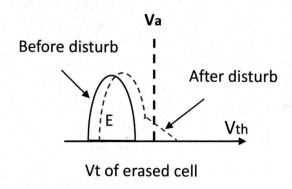

Figure 7-3. *Program disturb*

Write Amplification

Write amplification is another important concept in SSD firmware design. Because an SSD cannot overwrite data directly, each write operation requires a block to be erased first. This can result in a situation where the amount of data written to the drive is greater than the amount of data actually being stored, a phenomenon known as write amplification. SSD firmware includes algorithms to minimize write amplification, such as by using compression and deduplication to reduce the amount of data that needs to be written to the drive.

Factors that can affect the write amplification factor (WAF) include garbage-collection processes, which involve moving data around within the SSD to make space for new data, and the frequent storage of firmware management data in the NAND memory of the SSD, which can lead to additional data writes. A higher WAF indicates more data is being written to the SSD than was originally written by the host, leading to reduced performance and a shortened lifespan for the SSD. Meanwhile, a lower WAF indicates more-efficient data writing, resulting in better performance and a longer lifespan for the SSD.

The write amplification factor (WAF) is calculated by dividing the amount of data written to the SSD by the amount of data written by the host (see Figure 7-4). A WAF of 1 indicates that there is no write amplification, meaning that the amount of data written to the SSD is equal to the amount of data written by the host. A WAF greater than 1 indicates that the SSD has written more data to the disk than was written by the host, resulting in write amplification. For example, if an SSD writes 8 GB of data to the disk and the host writes 2 GB of data, the WAF would be 4, indicating significant write amplification. But if the SSD writes 5 GB of data and the host writes 5 GB of data, the WAF would be 1, indicating no write amplification.

$$WAF = \frac{\text{Data written to SSD}}{\text{Data written by host}}$$

Figure 7-4. *Write amplification factor*

Over-provisioning

Over-provisioning is the practice of allocating more memory to an SSD than is actually needed for user data. This can provide a number of benefits, including improved performance and increased endurance. SSD firmware can take advantage of over-provisioning by using the extra memory for wear leveling and garbage collection, which can help extend the lifespan of the drive.

It is the difference between the physical capacity of the flash memory and the logical capacity presented through the operating system (OS) as available for the user. During the garbage-collection, wear-leveling, and bad block–mapping operations on the SSD, the additional space from over-provisioning helps lower the write amplification when the controller writes to the flash memory. Over-provisioning is represented as a percentage ratio of extra capacity to user-available capacity, as seen in Figure 7-5.

$$OP = \frac{\text{physical capacity - user capacity}}{\text{user capacity}}$$

Figure 7-5. *Over-provisioning calculation*

Encryption

Self-encrypting drives (SEDs) are a type of SSD that uses hardware-based encryption to secure data at rest. One of the main benefits of SEDs is that they provide a secure and efficient way to protect data from unauthorized access. SEDs use hardware-based encryption to encrypt data as it is written to the drive, and they decrypt it as it is read. This means that the data is always encrypted while it is stored on the drive, and it cannot be accessed without the correct password or key.

There are several technologies and standards used to implement SEDs in SSD firmware. The most common of these is the Advanced Encryption Standard (AES). One of the challenges of implementing SEDs in SSD firmware is that they can have a negative impact on performance. Encrypting and decrypting data are tasks that require additional processing resources, which can slow down the drive and reduce its overall performance. To mitigate this impact, SSD manufacturers can optimize their firmware to minimize the overhead of encryption and decryption, or use hardware acceleration to offload these tasks onto dedicated hardware.

Summary

In summary, SSD firmware is a complex and critical component of an SSD, responsible for managing the various processes involved in storing and retrieving data, ensuring data integrity, and optimizing the performance of the drive. By understanding concepts such as wear leveling, garbage collection, data retention, program disturbance, error handling, write amplification, and over-provisioning, we can better appreciate the engineering that goes into creating reliable and high-performance storage devices.

CHAPTER 8

SSD Firmware Design Considerations

In this chapter, we will discuss the design considerations for solid-state drive (SSD) firmware. We will start by discussing the different types of SSDs and their requirements. We will then discuss the different components of SSD firmware and how they interact with each other. We will also discuss the different challenges that need to be addressed in the design of SSD firmware.

Design Considerations

1. SSD host interface: SATA, NVME, SAS, USB, etc.

2. Cache (RAM) memory availability:

    - To transfer data to/from host/SSD

    - Mapping table

3. Number of processors and their internal memory availability

4. Number of NAND channel supports

© Gopi Kuppan Thirumalai 2023
G. Kuppan Thirumalai, *A Beginner's Guide to SSD Firmware*,
https://doi.org/10.1007/978-1-4842-9888-6_8

5. Type of NAND used, characteristics, and limitations: SLC, MLC

- Limited number of program/erase cycles (SLC: 100,000, TLC: 3,000, QLC: 1,000)

- Erase block-wise, write page-wise; erase before write.

6. Performance requirements

7. Benchmark requirements

At a high level, an SSD operates by using a series of memory chips to store data. These memory chips are organized into pages and blocks, with each page typically able to store around 16 kilobytes (KB) of data and each block consisting of multiple pages. In order to write data to an SSD, the firmware must first erase the designated block. This is necessary because NAND flash memory cells can only be written to if they are in the erased state. After the erase operation is complete, write the pages within the block in a sequential order. Recall that this serves as a basic foundation on which we can build.

Once a page has been written to, it cannot be overwritten directly. Instead, the firmware must first erase the block that the page is a part of, which will also erase all of the other pages in the block. Rather than erasing and rewriting the same block, a new erased block should be chosen with a similar P/E (program/erase) cycle. This process is known as wear leveling and is used to ensure that all of the blocks in a die have been written to an equal number of times, thus extending the lifespan of the SSD.

One of the key components of SSD firmware is the *mapping table*, which is used to keep track of the location of data on the drive. The mapping table maps logical block addresses (LBAs) to physical block addresses (PBAs), which represent the location of data on the drive. When data is written to the drive, the SSD firmware uses the mapping table to determine the location where the data should be stored.

When data is read from an SSD, the firmware uses the mapping table to determine the physical block where the data is stored. The firmware then retrieves the data from the physical block and sends it back to the host device.

One of the key challenges in designing SSD firmware is ensuring that it is able to efficiently manage the various processes involved in storing and retrieving data. This includes optimizing the wear-leveling algorithm to minimize the number of times that blocks have to be erased, as well as managing the mapping table to ensure that data can be retrieved quickly.

Another important aspect of SSD firmware is ensuring data integrity. Because an SSD has no moving parts, it is less susceptible to physical damage than a traditional hard-disk drive (HDD). However, SSDs can still fail due to a variety of factors, including the failure of memory chips or the corruption of data. To protect against data loss, SSD firmware typically includes error-correcting code (ECC) and other mechanisms to detect and correct errors.

Unexpected Shutdown

An unexpected shutdown in an SSD occurs when the power to the device is unexpectedly interrupted while the device is in operation. This can happen due to power outages, surges, spikes, sags, or brownouts, as well as by manually removing the SSD from the system while it is powered on. What happens to data in transit to the SSD when there is an unexpected power interruption is an item overlooked by many industrial Original Equipment Manufacturer (OEM) host system designers. Limiting the system's exposure to data loss should be high on the list of design priorities.

This power loss will not cause issues during an idle or read operation, but if a write operation is occurring, there is the potential for some data loss or worse. Power loss during a write is also known as Write Abort. The main consequences of an unexpected shutdown during a write operation are file-system corruptions and internal device data corruption.

File-system corruptions occur when the operating system is unable to update the file-system records before the power is lost. Most operating systems will perform a file-system repair operation on the next power-up. Or it can typically be repaired by running a command or utility on the next power-up.

Internal device data corruption is more severe, as it can result in the entire flash drive's becoming unusable due to the corruption of the SSD's internal metadata, requiring a low-level format, which results in the loss of all data on the drive. To minimize the risk of data loss due to an unexpected shutdown, system designers should, in the design process, prioritize recovering the system effectively after such events.

One option is to take frequent recovery points and implement algorithms to find and restore data up until the restore point. Additionally, a special algorithm can be implemented to find the last page that was successfully written in a block. This can help protect against power interruptions and reduce the risk of data loss without the use of capacitors, which are often used to provide a temporary power source during unexpected shutdowns. By implementing these measures in the SSD firmware, designers can effectively address the issue of unexpected power loss and ensure the integrity of data in transit to the solid-state drive.

Power-Loss Protection

To effectively handle unexpected shutdowns and protect against data loss, designers have several options. One approach is to use power-loss protection capacitors in the hardware design of the SSD firmware. These capacitors provide a temporary power source in the event of an unexpected power loss, allowing the firmware to complete any in-progress writes and save any buffered data to the NAND.

In enterprise computing, data-loss protection is considered to be much more critical than it is in client computing. During an unexpected power loss, the SSD firmware can detect the power loss using hardware support and take steps to ensure all the unsaved data in the SSD is saved to maintain the integrity of data. This may include completing any in-progress writes to lower or upper pages (TLC), dumping buffered writes from non-volatile memory into the NAND (using SLC for faster write speed), or using hold-up circuitry to preserve enough time and energy to save the Flash Translation Layer (FTL) mapping table and other un-flushed data to the NAND.

Power-Loss Design Considerations

The power-loss protection mechanism in SSD firmware is a vital aspect of ensuring data integrity and preserving content metadata during unexpected power failures. While the volatile RAM translation table facilitates fast data access and updates during normal SSD operation, it is susceptible to data loss in the event of power loss. To address this challenge, the firmware adopts a proactive approach by utilizing persistent data structures stored in the non-volatile NAND flash array. These data structures contain essential content metadata and enable the reconstruction of the translation table during the next drive initialization. The firmware employs error protection mechanisms such as error-correcting codes (ECC) to safeguard the stored metadata from potential corruption. During the power-loss handling process, the firmware detects power loss, stores content metadata in the NAND flash array either alongside user data or in a separate block, and subsequently reconstructs the volatile RAM translation table on SSD initialization. This comprehensive power-loss protection mechanism ensures data reliability, minimizes data loss risks, and contributes to the robustness and efficiency of SSDs.

Individual modules need to maintain persistent data for simplicity and efficient operation. To ensure data integrity and recoverability, this persistent data is periodically saved from volatile RAM to the non-volatile NAND flash at restore points. Each module is responsible for updating its respective data structures, allocated in designated sections in RAM. Restore points can be created after the first boot, following an unexpected shutdown, when the persistent data buffer is full, or in response to program errors.

During restoration after an unexpected shutdown, minimizing the read time for persistent data from NAND is crucial to achieve faster boot times. Hence, efficient data-retrieval mechanisms should be employed. Regardless of whether the shutdown was safe or unsafe, during every subsequent boot, all restore-point data structures should be restored to their previous state, ensuring the system's consistent operation. To safeguard against data corruption, these data blocks should be protected by robust error-protection mechanisms, such as error-correcting codes (ECCs).

In extreme scenarios, if error correction fails, the device should still be able to boot, albeit in a read-only (RO) mode, ensuring that the data remains intact and is not subjected to further risks. The combination of efficient restore points, error protection, and robust recovery mechanisms ensures the reliability and resilience of the system in handling unexpected events and contributes to an overall improved user experience.

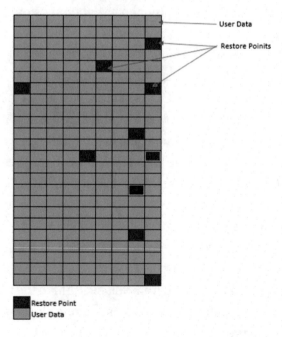

Figure 8-1. *System restore point for unexpected shutdown handling*

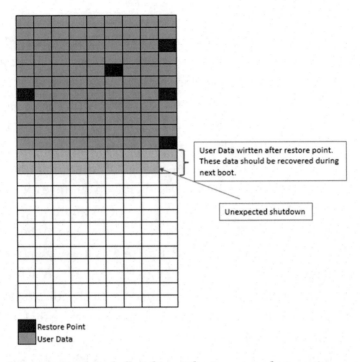

User Data wirtten after restore point.
These data should be recovered during
next boot.

Unexpected shutdown

■ Restore Point
■ User Data

Figure 8-2. *Unexpected shutdown during user data write*

The design considerations of SSD firmware are a complex process that involves optimizing various algorithms and data structures in order to maximize the performance and reliability of the drive.

Best Practices for Optimizing and Maintaining SSD Firmware

Next we will examine some key concepts for optimizing and maintaining SSD firmware, including reducing DRAM (dynamic random access memory, volatile memory) access, minimizing the code in the critical path of read and write operations, and managing firmware state snapshots. As fellow programmers, it is important that you understand the best practices for optimizing and maintaining SSD firmware. SSDs are becoming increasingly popular, and their firmware is complex. SSD firmware can have a significant impact on performance, reliability, and security. By following best practices, programmers can develop firmware that is more efficient, reliable, secure, and user-friendly.

One of the key considerations for optimizing SSD firmware is reducing the number of accesses to the DRAM on the drive. DRAM is a type of memory that is used by the SSD to store data temporarily, but accessing it can be slow and consume a significant amount of power. By reducing the number of accesses to the DRAM, it is possible to improve the performance of the SSD and reduce its power consumption.

One way to reduce DRAM access is to include less code in the critical path of read and write operations. The critical path is the sequence of operations that are performed when data is being read from or written to the drive. By reducing the amount of code in the critical path, it is possible to speed up these operations and reduce the amount of time that the drive spends accessing the DRAM.

Another approach to reducing DRAM access is to schedule read operations for data maintenance tasks, such as garbage collection and wear leveling. By performing these tasks during times when the drive is not being heavily used, it is possible to reduce their impact on the performance of the drive and minimize the number of accesses to the DRAM.

In addition to reducing DRAM access, it is also important to manage the firmware state snapshot data (management data). The firmware state snapshot is a copy of the firmware that is stored on the drive and is used to restore the firmware in the event of a failure. By managing this data carefully—i.e., keeping the management data as small as possible and writing only when necessary and when firmware is idle—it is possible to reduce the amount of space that is used by the firmware state snapshot, which can help to improve the overall performance and reliability of the drive.

Summary

In conclusion, optimizing and maintaining SSD firmware requires a careful balance of performance, power consumption, and reliability. By focusing on reducing DRAM access, minimizing the code in the critical path of read and write operations, and managing the firmware state snapshot data, it is possible to create SSD firmware that is optimized for performance and reliability.

CHAPTER 9

Flash Translation Layer (FTL)

The flash translation layer (FTL) is a key component of the firmware in a NAND-based solid-state drive (SSD). It is responsible for managing the interaction between the host computer and the underlying NAND chips, and it plays a crucial role in the performance and reliability of the SSD.

The FTL is implemented as a layer of software that sits between the host computer and the NAND chips, and it serves several key functions: mapping table, bad block management, wear leveling, and garbage collection. These algorithms and data structures are designed to optimize the performance and reliability of the SSD, and they are constantly updated and refined as the SSD is used.

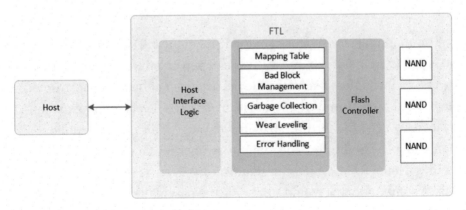

Figure 9-1. *FTL block diagram*

© Gopi Kuppan Thirumalai 2023
G. Kuppan Thirumalai, *A Beginner's Guide to SSD Firmware*,
https://doi.org/10.1007/978-1-4842-9888-6_9

Mapping Table

The FTL is responsible for mapping logical block addresses (LBAs) used by the host to the physical pages and blocks on the NAND chips (physical block address; PBA). This allows the host to access data on the SSD using logical addresses, rather than having to know the specific physical location of each block on the NAND chips. The data structure can simply be an array, where the index is LBA and its value is PBA. This address translation is necessary to ensure that data is correctly mapped to the physical locations within the NAND flash memory. The FTL (flash translation layer) acts as an intermediary to perform this translation.

Table 9-1. *Basic Mapping Table*

LBA	PBA
0	0x1243
1	0x3953
. .	. .
100	0x9324

This mapping table is stored in the RAM of the SSD for speed of access and is persisted in flash memory in case of power failure. When the SSD powers up, the table is read from the persisted version and reconstructed into the RAM. The simple approach is to use page-level mapping to map any logical page from the host to a physical page. This mapping policy offers a lot of flexibility, but the major drawback is that the mapping table requires a lot of RAM, which can significantly increase the manufacturing costs. A solution to that would store only the part of the table required to service the read request from the host in RAM. The disadvantage of this approach would be needing to read from NAND (on demand) if the host read does not have a mapping table in RAM. This will have an impact on random read performance.

A logical-to-physical block address table (mapping table) is an essential component of SSD firmware. It is used to translate logical block addresses (LBAs) used by the host system to physical block addresses (PBAs) on the SSD. The mapping table is necessary because the physical blocks on an SSD may wear out or become faulty over time, and the firmware must be able to remap logical blocks to new physical blocks to maintain the integrity of the data.

Size of the Mapping Table

The size of the mapping table depends on the capacity of the SSD and the addressing scheme used. In larger-capacity SSDs, the mapping table can be substantial due to the increased number of LBAs and corresponding PBAs. For example, a mapping table for a multi-terabyte SSD can contain millions of entries.

Size of SSD: 128 GB

Number of clusters: Assuming each cluster is 4 KB (4 kilobytes), let's calculate the number of clusters:

134,217,728 KB (SSD size) / 4 KB (cluster size) = 33,554,432 clusters

Assuming each mapping table entry requires 4 bytes to store the corresponding PBA (physical block address), we can calculate the total RAM size required for the mapping table as follows:

Total RAM size required for mapping table = Number of clusters * Number of bytes required to store the PBA

Total RAM size required = 33,554,432 clusters * 4 bytes = 134,217,728 bytes

Therefore, for an SSD with a size of 128 GB and a cluster size of 4 KB, the mapping table would require approximately 134,217,728 bytes or 134 megabytes of RAM to store the mapping entries.

Storing the Mapping Table in RAM

Ideally, it would be advantageous to store the entire mapping table in random access memory (RAM) for fast access. However, due to the limitations of RAM capacity in most SSD designs (due to cost), it is often impractical or impossible to load the complete mapping table into memory. Instead, SSD firmware employs strategies to optimize the storage of the mapping table. For example, a mapping table for a multi-terabyte SSD can contain millions or even billions of entries.

Partial Loading of the Mapping Table

To overcome RAM limitations, the mapping table is typically loaded partially into RAM, focusing on the frequently accessed portions. The FTL prioritizes loading the mapping entries required for active LBAs, ensuring efficient and quick access to frequently accessed data. This partial loading strategy allows the SSD to maintain acceptable performance while conserving valuable RAM resources.

Storage of Non-Loaded Mapping Entries

The mapping entries that are not loaded into RAM reside in the NAND flash memory. These entries are accessed on an as-needed basis. When an LBA that is not in the loaded portion of the mapping table needs to be accessed, the FTL utilizes algorithms to locate the corresponding mapping entry in the NAND flash memory. This retrieval process may introduce some additional latency due to the need to access the slower NAND storage.

Write/Update Operations and the Mapping Table

During write/update operations, the mapping table undergoes modifications to accommodate new LBAs and PBAs that result from data writes, garbage collection, and wear leveling. To optimize the write/update process, SSD firmware employs various techniques, including maintaining a dirty cache buffer of the mapping table in RAM.

Dirty Cache Buffer in RAM

A common approach is to utilize a portion of RAM as a cache buffer for the mapping table. This buffer temporarily holds the mapping table entries, which are modified before they are flushed back to the NAND flash memory. The dirty cache buffer allows for efficient and quick updates without constantly writing to the NAND, which can be time-consuming.

Write/Update Process with Dirty Cache Buffer

When a write/update operation occurs, the SSD firmware first checks the dirty cache buffer in RAM. If the mapping table entry for the specific LBA already exists in the dirty cache buffer, it is updated directly in RAM, avoiding unnecessary writes to the NAND flash memory. This approach reduces latency and improves overall performance.

Flush to NAND

To ensure data durability and to prevent loss in the event of a power failure or system crash, the contents of the dirty cache buffer need to be periodically flushed back to the NAND flash memory. This flushing process involves writing the modified mapping table entries from the dirty cache buffer to their corresponding locations in the NAND. The frequency of flushing can vary based on factors such as the size of the dirty cache buffer and the SSD firmware's internal policies.

Mapping Table Management and Optimization

As the SSD operates, the mapping table undergoes continuous updates to accommodate new LBAs and PBAs resulting from write operations, garbage collection, and wear leveling. Efficient management of the mapping table involves carefully balancing the usage of RAM resources, the frequency of flush operations, and the optimization of write/update processes. SSD firmware employs various techniques, like buffering, compression, and intelligent mapping algorithms, to optimize mapping-table management, reduce write amplification, and improve overall SSD performance.

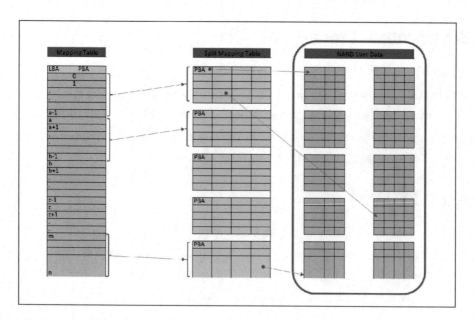

Figure 9-2. *Multi-level mapping table*

The following is a step-by-step guide on how the mapping table is created, accessed, and updated in the erase, read, and write path of an SSD:

> **Initialization:** When the SSD is first initialized, the firmware creates a blank mapping table. This table consists of a series of entries, each of which maps a logical block address to a physical block address. Initially, all of these entries are set to a default value, indicating that the logical block has not yet been mapped to a physical block.

Table 9-2. *Mapping Table: Init*

LBA	PBA
0	0xFFFF
1	0xFFFF
.	.
.	.
100	0xFFFF

> **Write:** When the host system writes data to the SSD, it sends a write command to the SSD along with the LBA and the data to be written. The firmware receives this command and determines which physical block to write to. Then, it sends the data to be written to that block and updates the mapping table accordingly.
>
> FTL performs a process called *block allocation*, which involves selecting a suitable physical block to store the data and updating the mapping table

135

to reflect the new mapping. This process takes into account factors such as wear leveling, bad block management, and optimizing data placement to enhance performance and longevity.

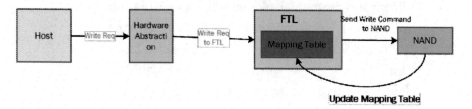

Figure *9-3.* *Mapping table update during write path*

Table *9-3.* *Mapping Table after Write*

LBA	PBA
0	0x1243
1	0x3953
.	.
.	.
100	0x9324

Read: When the host system reads data from the SSD, it sends a read command to the SSD along with the LBA of the data to be read. The firmware receives this command and looks up the corresponding entry in the mapping table. If the entry is set to the default value, the firmware returns an error to the host system indicating that the requested data is not present on the SSD (unmapped data). If the entry is set to a physical block, the firmware reads the data from that physical block and returns it to the host system.

Table 9-4. *Mapping Table*
While Read

LBA	PBA
0	0x1243
1	0x3953
. .	. .
100	0x9324

Garbage Collection: As physical blocks on the SSD wear out or become faulty, during garbage collection the firmware may need to update the mapping table to remap logical blocks to new physical blocks. Figure 9-4 shows an example of how a physical block is written, unmapped, and moved to a new physical block and the mapping table being updated in parallel.

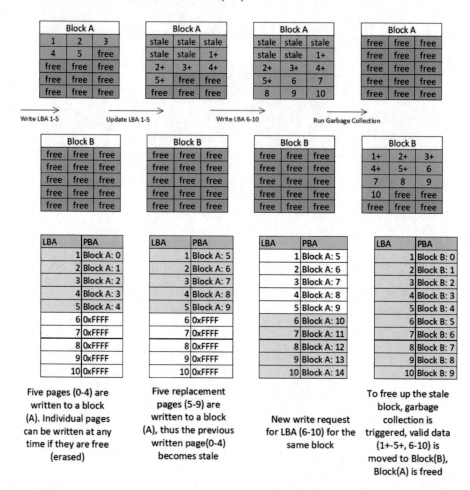

Figure 9-4. *Garbage collection for two SSD storage blocks—Block A and Block B—as they progress through the data update mapping table process*

> **Physical Erase/Sanitize/Format:** When the SSD firmware receives an erase command, it selects the physical block specified in the command and erases it by setting all the bits in the block to 1. This allows the block to be overwritten with new data.

The firmware also updates the corresponding entry in the mapping table to reflect the fact that the logical block address is now mapped to an erased physical block.

Table 9-5. *Mapping Table after Physical Erase/Sanitize*

LBA	PBA
0	0xFFFF
1	0xFFFF
. .	. .
100	0xFFFF

Trim: When the SSD firmware receives a trim command, it marks the specified logical block address as no longer in use. This may involve updating the corresponding entries in the mapping table to set them to the default value, indicating that the logical blocks are not currently mapped to any physical blocks. The trim operation does not actually erase the physical blocks associated with the logical blocks; rather, it simply informs the SSD that these blocks are no longer needed and should be erased at a later time.

This can improve the performance of writing data to SSDs and help extend the lifespan of the SSD. TRIM is available for SSDs that support the Serial ATA (SATA) interface, while the UNMAP command serves a similar purpose for Small Computer System Interface (SCSI)

SSDs, and the DEALLOCATE operation performs a similar function in the nonvolatile memory express (NVMe) command set for Peripheral Component Interconnect Express SSDs.

The TRIM command works by enabling the operating system to proactively notify the SSD which data pages in a particular block can be erased. This allows the SSD's controller to manage the available storage space more efficiently for data. TRIM eliminates any unnecessary copying of discarded or invalid data pages during the garbage-collection process, which is an internal SSD housekeeping operation that manages and maintains available storage space by moving valid data pages to another block on the SSD so that the original block containing invalid data pages can be erased. By reducing the number of data pages that need to be moved during garbage collection, TRIM can reduce the number of program/erase cycles (P/E cycles) to the NAND flash media and extend the endurance of the SSD.

Using TRIM can provide benefits in terms of performance and drive longevity. It can speed up the write performance of the drive by avoiding unnecessary copying of invalid data and extend the lifespan of the drive by reducing the number of erase cycles.

Table 9-6. *Mapping Table after Trim*

LBA	PBA
0	0xFFFF
1	0x3953
.	.
.	.
100	0x9324

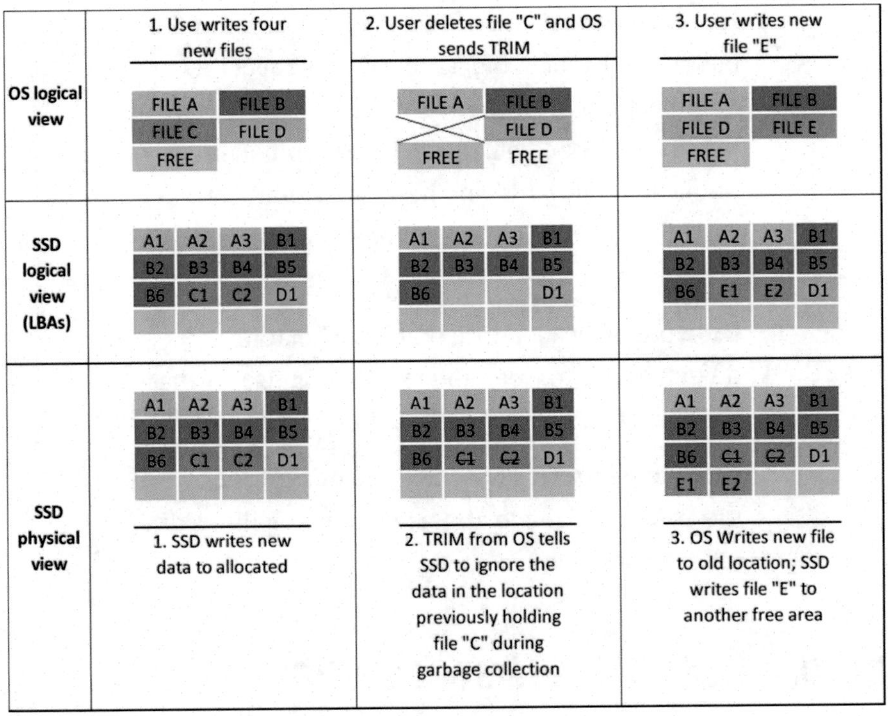

	1. Use writes four new files	2. User deletes file "C" and OS sends TRIM	3. User writes new file "E"
OS logical view	FILE A FILE B FILE C FILE D FREE	FILE A FILE B 　　　 FILE D FREE FREE	FILE A FILE B FILE D FILE E FREE
SSD logical view (LBAs)	A1 A2 A3 B1 B2 B3 B4 B5 B6 C1 C2 D1	A1 A2 A3 B1 B2 B3 B4 B5 B6 　 　 D1	A1 A2 A3 B1 B2 B3 B4 B5 B6 E1 E2 D1
SSD physical view	A1 A2 A3 B1 B2 B3 B4 B5 B6 C1 C2 D1 1. SSD writes new data to allocated	A1 A2 A3 B1 B2 B3 B4 B5 B6 C1 C2 D1 2. TRIM from OS tells SSD to ignore the data in the location previously holding file "C" during garbage collection	A1 A2 A3 B1 B2 B3 B4 B5 B6 C1 C2 D1 E1 E2 3. OS Writes new file to old location; SSD writes file "E" to another free area

Figure 9-5. *Trim execution flow from host*

Bad Block Management

Bad blocks on an SSD can be a major problem, as they can prevent the device from functioning properly and may result in data loss. To address this issue, the firmware on an SSD includes a feature called bad block management, which is responsible for identifying and remapping bad blocks on the NAND chips, which are blocks that can no longer be reliably written to or read from due to physical defects or damage.

There are three types of bad blocks that the firmware may encounter:

1. *Factory-marked bad blocks:* Bad blocks (or initial bad blocks), that is, blocks that do not meet the manufacturer's standards or have been tested by the manufacturer and fail to meet the manufacturer's published standards, and have been identified as bad blocks by the manufacturer when they leave the factory.

2. *Used bad blocks:* Those that have become defective due to wear and tear during use, or that have reached the end of their lifespan.

3. *False bad blocks:* Those that are misjudged by the controller due to abnormal power failures or other issues.

Factory Bad Block Assessment

When a specific physical block in the NAND flash memory is detected as defective (bad block), the firmware must perform two fundamental activities: record the flash address of the bad block and update the bad block bitmap table.

Bad Block Flash Address

A bad block flash address contains essential information about the physical block that is considered defective. The exact format/content of this address depends on the NAND flash manufacturer. The firmware needs this information to translate the flash address information into meaningful data and to manage logical block mappings accurately.

Recording Bad Block Flash Address

The firmware must promptly record the flash address of the detected bad block. This information will be crucial in managing and avoiding future access to the defective block during normal read and write operations. The firmware should include protective measures to prevent any write or erase commands from targeting these identified defective blocks. Attempting to perform erase or program operations on such defective blocks will yield unpredictable and indeterminate results.

Initial Bad Block Handling Flow

When an SSD is powered up and mounted for the first time, the firmware performs the initial bad block handling to identify and manage any factory-marked defective physical blocks in the NAND flash memory. The goal is to ensure that these bad blocks are appropriately marked and avoided during subsequent read and write operations to maintain data integrity and optimize SSD performance.

Step 1: Power-Up and Mounting

The SSD is powered up, and the firmware initializes the device.

During the mounting process, the firmware initializes the bad block management mechanism, including the bad block bitmap table.

Step 2: Reading the NAND Flash

As part of the initialization process, the firmware reads each block in the NAND flash memory. The firmware checks for any errors or anomalies during the read operation.

Step 3: Identifying Bad Blocks

If a read operation encounters a defective physical block (bad block), the firmware identifies it as a bad block and records the flash address of the bad block in a bad block bitmap.

Step 4: Updating Bad Block Bitmap

After identifying a bad block, the firmware updates the corresponding entry in the bitmap table, indicating that the block is defective.

Step 5: Skipping Bad Blocks

During subsequent read and write operations, the firmware checks the bad block bitmap table. When accessing data, the firmware will skip any blocks marked as bad in the bitmap table, effectively avoiding the defective physical blocks.

Step 6: Error Handling (Optional)

If the bad block causes any data corruption or errors during the read operation, the firmware may implement error correction techniques or take appropriate measures to ensure data integrity.

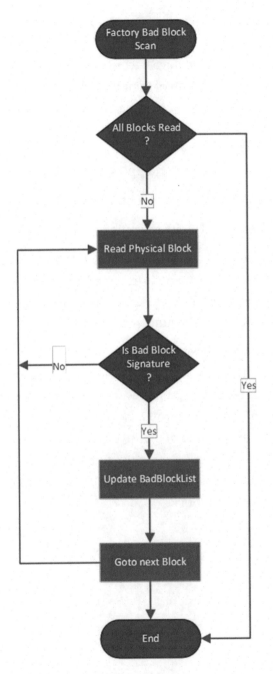

Figure 9-6. *Initial bad block scan flow*

Used Bad Block Assessment

Used bad blocks are those that have become defective due to wear and tear or that have reached the end of their lifespan. The firmware on an SSD is responsible for identifying used bad blocks and managing them to maintain the reliability and performance of the device. During program or erase actions, if the status register of the operation fails, the SSD controller will list this block as a bad block. Examples are as follows:

- An error occurred while executing the erase command.

- An error occurred while executing the write command.

- When the read command is executed, an error occurs; when the read command is executed, if the number of bit errors exceeds the error-correction capability of the ECC, the block will be judged as a bad block.

To keep track of bad blocks, SSDs have a feature called a bad block able (BBT), which is typically stored in a separate area of the NAND memory. The BBT is read after each power-up to make it more efficient, and it may also be backed up to protect against damage to the NAND memory. The number of copies of the BBT that are backed up may vary depending on the specific design strategy, with some SSDs backing up with as many as eight copies. Figures 9-7 and 9-8 show basic (not the only way) handling for used bad blocks.

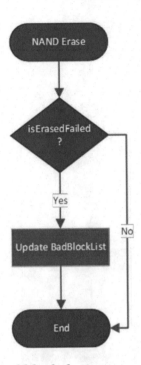

Figure 9-7. *Handling bad block during erase operation*

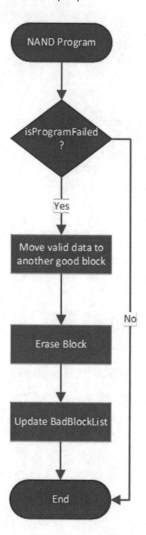

Figure 9-8. *Handling bad block during NAND program operation*

There are generally two approaches to managing bad blocks: the bad block skip strategy and the bad block replacement strategy. The bad block skip strategy involves simply skipping over any bad blocks and not using them, while the bad block replacement strategy involves replacing bad blocks with good ones. Both approaches have their own benefits and drawbacks, and the choice of which to use may depend on the specific requirements of the SSD.

Bad Block Skipping Strategy

1. For the initial bad block, the bad block skip will skip the corresponding bad block through BBT and directly store the data in the next good block.

2. For the new bad block, update the bad block to the BBT, transfer the valid data in the bad block to the next good block, and skip this bad block every time you do the corresponding read, program, or erase in the future.

Bad Block Replacement Strategy

In general, the OP (over provision)-area free block is used to replace the new block during use. Take garbage collection as an example. When the garbage-collection mechanism is running, the valid page data in the block that needs to be reclaimed is first moved to the free block, and then the erase operation is performed on the block. It is assumed that the erase status register is fed back at this time. When the erase fails, the bad block management mechanism will update the block address to the new bad block list, and at the same time write the valid data pages in the bad block to the free block in the OP area. It will update the bad block management table, and next time when writing data, it will skip the bad block and go directly to the next available block.

The OP size varies from manufacturer to manufacturer; there are different application scenarios, different reliability requirements, and different OP sizes. There is a trade-off between OP and stability. The larger the OP, the larger the available space for garbage collection in the process of continuous writing, the more stable the performance, and the smoother the performance curve. Conversely, the smaller the OP, the worse the performance stability, the larger the available space for users, and the lower the cost.

Generally speaking, OP can be set to 5 percent to 50 percent. An OP of 7 percent is a common ratio. Unlike the 2 percent fixed block suggested by the manufacturer, 7 percent is not a fixed block for OP. Instead, it is dynamically distributed among all blocks, which is more conducive to the wear-leveling strategy.

Summary

In summary, the FTL is a critical component of the firmware in a NAND-based SSD, and it plays a vital role in managing the interaction between the host and the NAND chips. It is responsible for ensuring that data is stored and retrieved efficiently, and it helps to maintain the performance and reliability of the SSD over time.

CHAPTER 10

User Data Flow

In this chapter, we will discuss the user data flow in solid-state drive (SSD) firmware. We will start by discussing the write path, which is the process of writing data from the host to the NAND flash memory. We will then discuss the read path, which is the process of reading data from the NAND flash memory and transferring it back to the host.

Write Path

In SSD firmware, the *write path* refers to the process of writing data from the host to the NAND flash memory. When the host sends a write request command, the device allocates a cache buffer to receive the data. The data is then transferred from the host to the device cache, where it is transformed and prepared for writing to the NAND memory by the firmware translation layer (FTL). This process includes adding error-correcting codes (ECCs) to the data to ensure its integrity.

Once the data has been prepared for writing, the FTL programs it into the NAND memory. When the program is completed successfully, it updates the mapping table with the physical block address (PBA) for the corresponding logical block addresses (LBAs) that were successfully written. The goal of this process is to achieve the maximum write performance by ensuring that the NAND throughput is utilized to its full potential.

© Gopi Kuppan Thirumalai 2023
G. Kuppan Thirumalai, *A Beginner's Guide to SSD Firmware*,
https://doi.org/10.1007/978-1-4842-9888-6_10

To achieve this goal, the FTL arranges and performs independent tasks on the write path in parallel on different threads or CPUs, and sequences the NAND programming while preparing the next set of NAND programming. It also arranges the data for programming in a way that is most optimal for NAND operations, such as by using multi-plane and multi-die techniques to maximize channel and die capacity.

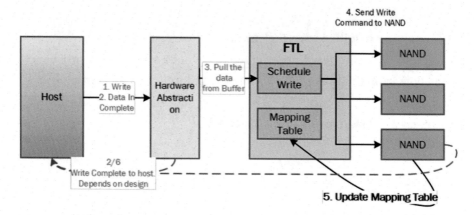

Figure 10-1.   *Host write data path*

Read Path

The *read path* refers to the process of reading data from the NAND flash memory and transferring back to the host. This is a critical path in the system, as the host expects the device to read data with low latency.

The read process begins when the host issues a read command, which is processed by the FTL. The FTL translates the logical block address (LBA) of the requested data into a physical block address (PBA), and then sends a NAND read command to the PBA. The FTL monitors the progress of the read command and transfers the data from the NAND cache buffer to a read buffer inside the flash controller.

If the data is found to be error-free, it is transferred from the read buffer to the SSD cache. From there, it is transferred to the host. If the data needs to be corrected and is within the correction capability of the SSD firmware, it is corrected before being transferred to the host.

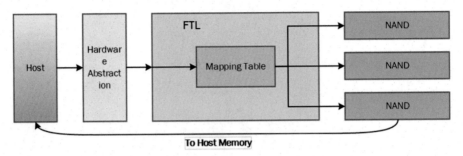

Figure 10-2. *Host data read path*

Overall, the write and read paths in SSD firmware are complex processes that involve a series of steps to ensure the efficient and reliable reading of data to and from the NAND memory. By optimizing these processes and carefully managing the data transfer, SSD manufacturers can improve the performance and reliability of their drives.

Summary

This chapter has discussed the user data flow in SSD firmware. We have seen how the write and read paths are two critical processes that ensure the efficient and reliable transfer of data between the host and the SSD. We have also seen how the SSD firmware can optimize these processes to improve the performance and reliability of the drive.

CHAPTER 11

Throttling

Throttling is a crucial feature in solid-state drive (SSD) firmware design. It aims to manage and regulate the drive's temperature and power consumption to ensure optimal performance, reliability, and data integrity. Excessive heat and power usage can lead to performance degradation and potential hardware damage. The SSD firmware incorporates intelligent throttling mechanisms to mitigate these risks and maintain efficient operation under varying workloads and environmental conditions.

Thermal Throttling

Temperature Monitoring

The firmware continuously monitors the SSD's temperature using onboard temperature sensors. When the temperature reaches predefined thresholds, the thermal throttling mechanism is triggered.

Throttling Mechanism

Upon detecting high temperatures, the firmware enacts thermal throttling, which reduces the SSD's operating frequency and performance to prevent overheating. This proactive approach prevents thermal-induced errors and prolongs the drive's lifespan.

© Gopi Kuppan Thirumalai 2023
G. Kuppan Thirumalai, *A Beginner's Guide to SSD Firmware*,
https://doi.org/10.1007/978-1-4842-9888-6_11

Temperature Recovery

As the temperature decreases, the firmware gradually restores the SSD's operating frequency to normal levels. This adaptive approach ensures that the SSD efficiently manages temperature fluctuations while maximizing performance.

Design Consideration

Thermal throttling in SSD firmware involves the use of periodic credits to manage NAND access requests based on the temperature of the drive. The throttling module periodically monitors the temperature sensor using system support and determines the current throttling state. Based on this state, the module provides appropriate credit values to the flash controller module. These credits are consumed by the flash controller module while scheduling NAND access.

When the supplied credits are exhausted, the firmware must initiate a slowdown of all NAND operations to reduce the temperature. This is achieved by entering an idle mode where all ongoing operations are stalled, and the hardware remains in an idle state for the remaining period of the throttling cycle. During this time, the CPUs and hardware are in a sleep mode; they wake up at the start of the next thermal throttling cycle. This proactive approach prevents the drive from overheating, ensuring reliable performance and data integrity, even under challenging thermal conditions.

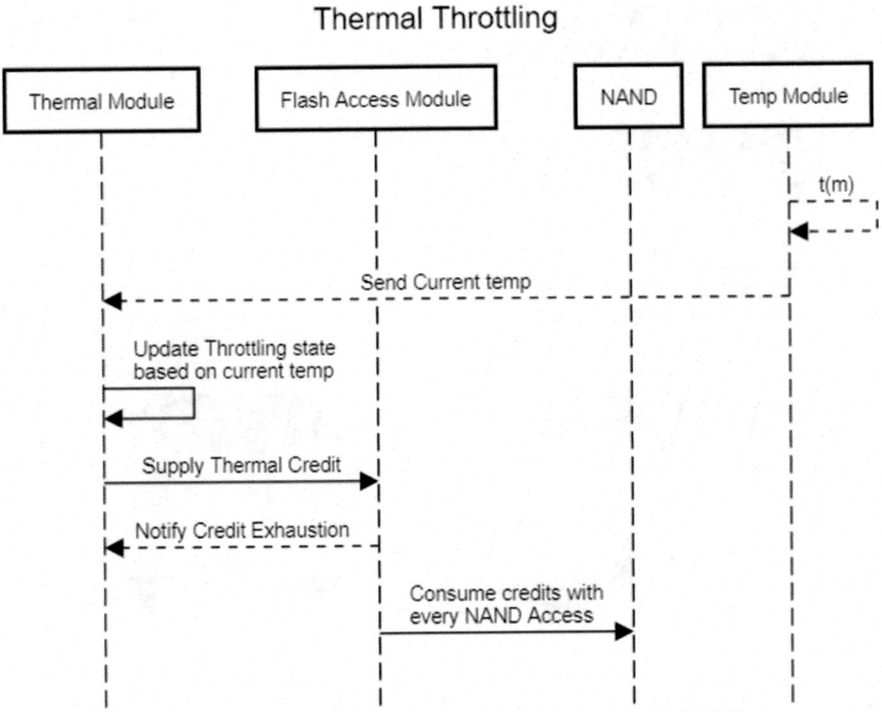

Thermal Throttling

Figure 11-1. *Thermal throttling sequence diagram*

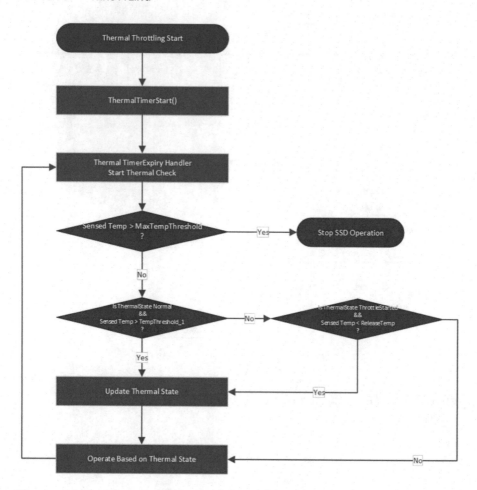

Figure 11-2. *Thermal throttling flow diagram*

Power Throttling

Power Monitoring

The firmware continuously monitors the SSD's power consumption. If the power consumption exceeds predefined thresholds, the power throttling mechanism is activated.

Throttling Mechanism

Upon reaching critical power levels, the firmware initiates power throttling, limiting the drive's power consumption. By doing so, the SSD avoids overloading power supplies and prevents potential data corruption or hardware damage.

Power Recovery

Once power consumption stabilizes within safe limits, the firmware gradually restores the SSD's power usage to normal levels. This adaptive approach ensures that the SSD operates efficiently under varying power conditions.

Combined Throttling

Synergistic Operation

Thermal and power throttling mechanisms can work in tandem. If the SSD encounters both high temperatures and excessive power usage simultaneously, the firmware optimizes the throttling strategy to address both issues effectively.

Priority Management

In cases where thermal and power constraints conflict, the firmware intelligently prioritizes the most critical aspect to ensure the SSD's continued operation with minimal risk.

Dynamic Performance Adjustments

Workload Awareness

The firmware dynamically adjusts throttling based on the SSD's workload. For demanding tasks, the drive may temporarily tolerate higher temperatures or more power consumption to maintain optimal performance. During low-intensity tasks, throttling may be more aggressive to conserve energy and reduce heat generation.

Logging and Reporting

Event Logging

The firmware maintains a log of thermal and power throttling events, providing visibility into the drive's operational conditions and any corrective actions taken.

Health Monitoring

The firmware also tracks and reports the drive's health status, which includes both thermal- and power-related metrics, to facilitate system monitoring and preventive maintenance.

Throttling is a crucial mechanism used to regulate NAND flash access and prevent potential overheating, power consumption, and performance issues. Understanding the principles and implementation of throttling is vital for engineers and developers working on solid-state drives and other NAND flash-based systems.

We began by exploring the different types of throttling, including thermal throttling and power throttling. Thermal throttling helps control NAND flash temperature by adjusting access rates based on temperature measurements. Meanwhile, power throttling efficiently manages power consumption during NAND flash operations to prevent excessive power draw.

Summary

In conclusion, understanding the intricacies of throttling in NAND flash is vital for optimizing the performance, reliability, and longevity of NAND flash-based systems. Engineers and developers must be well versed in implementing effective throttling strategies to ensure the smooth operation of devices and prevent potential damage or data loss due to excessive temperatures or power consumption.

CHAPTER 12

Exception Handling

In this chapter, we will discuss exception handling in solid-state drive (SSD) firmware. We will start by discussing the different types of errors that can occur in SSDs, such as read errors, program errors, and erase errors. We will then discuss how to handle these types of errors and how to mitigate them in SSD firmware.

Exception handling is an important aspect of SSD firmware development. SSDs are complex systems that are prone to various types of errors, including read errors, program errors, and erase errors. In this chapter, we will discuss how to handle these types of errors and how to mitigate them in SSD firmware.

Read Errors

Read errors occur when the SSD is unable to read data from the NAND flash memory cells. This can be caused by a variety of factors, such as defects in the NAND cells, interference from external sources, faulty hardware, or temperature variations during read operations. For example, broadening of VTH distributions due to noise can lead to read errors.

© Gopi Kuppan Thirumalai 2023
G. Kuppan Thirumalai, *A Beginner's Guide to SSD Firmware*,
https://doi.org/10.1007/978-1-4842-9888-6_12

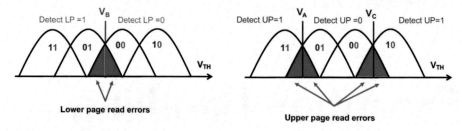

Figure 12-1. *Read error due to Vth distribution shift*

Handling

SSDs can fix NAND read errors by using special codes and techniques. These codes can help to identify and correct errors that occur when reading data from NAND memory. Other methods, such as retrying the read or adjusting the read voltage, may also be used to fix errors.

Another common approach to handling read errors in enterprise-level SSDs is to use a redundant array of independent disks (RAID) technology. RAID is a technique that involves grouping multiple SSDs together to form a single logical storage unit. The data on the SSDs is striped across the drives, which allows the SSDs to work together to improve performance and reliability. In the event of a read error on one of the SSDs, the data can be reconstructed from the other SSDs in the RAID group.

In addition to error-correcting code (ECC), wear-leveling algorithms, and RAID technology, there are a couple of other approaches to handling read errors in enterprise-level SSDs that are worth mentioning, as follows:

Reed-Solomon error correction: Reed-Solomon error correction is a technique that is similar to ECC, but it is more powerful and can correct a larger number of errors. It works by adding extra parity bits to the data, which can be used to detect and correct errors that occur when the data is read back from the SSD.

Low-density parity-check (LDPC) codes: LDPC codes are another type of error-correcting code that can be used to detect and correct errors in data stored on an SSD. LDPC codes are particularly effective at correcting errors that are caused by noise or interference in the data transmission process.

Program Errors

Program errors occur when the SSD is unable to write data to the NAND cells. This can be caused by a variety of factors, such as defects in the NAND cells, interference from external sources, faulty hardware, or P/E cycle reached.

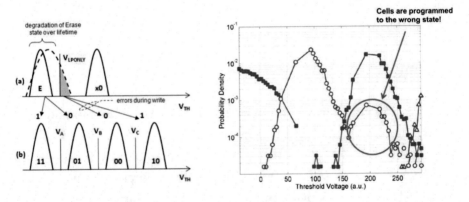

Figure 12-2. *Program error on MLC NAND flash*

Handling

To handle program errors, SSD firmware should include algorithms that can detect and recover from these errors. For example, the firmware may attempt to rewrite the data to a different location in the NAND memory, or it may use error-correcting codes to ensure that the data being written is accurate.

One approach is to continue writing until the end of the block is reached, and then move on to a new block while marking the old block as bad. Another option is to immediately stop writing the data and move to a new block, while also marking the old block as bad. These strategies allow the SSD firmware to minimize the impact of program errors and maintain the integrity of the data being written.

Program Abort

This scenario results from an unexpected power cycle while the NAND programming is in progress. Due to power loss, the NAND cells are left in the wrong/incomplete voltage distribution state and cannot be reprogrammed. Reading data from these cells may give uncorrectable error.

Handling

To handle program abort, the firmware needs to keep track of the status of each block and page. This is typically done through the use of a block management table (BMT) and a page management table (PMT). The BMT keeps track of the status of each block, including whether it is good or bad, and the PMT keeps track of the status of each page within a block.

When the firmware detects a program abort, it will first scan the BMT and PMT to determine the last successfully programmed page. It will then try to recover as much data as possible from the partially programmed page and move it to a new block. The old block will be closed and marked for garbage collection.

In addition to recovering data from a partially programmed page, the firmware may also need to recover data from other blocks that were affected by the power loss. This can be done by scanning the BMT and PMT to identify any blocks that were being erased or programmed at the time of the power loss. The data from these blocks can then be recovered and moved to new blocks as well. The firmware also updates the mapping table to reflect the new location of the recovered data.

Overall, handling program abort is an important aspect of SSD firmware design. By keeping track of the status of each block and page, the firmware can recover as much data as possible and ensure that the SSD continues to operate correctly after an unexpected power loss.

Erase Errors

Erase errors occur when the SSD is unable to erase data from the NAND cells. This can be caused by a variety of factors, such as defects in the NAND cells, interference from external sources, or faulty hardware.

Handling

To handle erase errors, SSD firmware should include algorithms that can detect and recover from these errors. For example, the firmware may attempt to erase the data from a different location in the NAND memory and mark the old block as bad.

To mitigate these types of errors, SSD firmware should be designed with robust error-handling and recovery algorithms. Additionally, SSD manufacturers can use high-quality NAND cells and carefully test their products to reduce the likelihood of errors' occurring. Finally, SSD firmware should be regularly updated to fix any known issues and improve error-handling and recovery capabilities.

Summary

This chapter has discussed exception handling in SSD firmware. We have seen how SSDs are prone to various types of errors, and how these errors can be handled by the firmware. We have also seen how the firmware can be designed to mitigate the likelihood of errors' occurring.

CHAPTER 13

Performance

In this chapter, we will discuss the performance of solid-state drives (SSDs). We will start by defining some of the key performance metrics, such as input/output operations per second (IOPS), throughput, and latency. We will then discuss the factors that can impact the performance of an SSD, such as the memory type, memory architecture, memory controller, and firmware. Finally, we will discuss some of the strategies that can be used to boost the performance of an SSD through firmware design and implementation.

SSD performance tests and benchmarking test SSD performance under a variety of workloads. SSD firmware engineers who want to monitor their drive can use benchmarks to observe read and write rates and other performance metrics under different conditions. Those read and write speeds can then be marketed to potential customers who are searching for persistent storage devices that provide quick access to data. An ideal benchmark test gives customers an accurate picture of how quickly they'll be able to access that data using the SSD.

The key performance criteria for an SSD include the following:

> **Transfer Speed:** This refers to the speed at which data can be transferred to or from the SSD. This can be measured in terms of read and write speeds, which are typically expressed in megabytes per second (MB/s) or gigabytes per second (GB/s).

© Gopi Kuppan Thirumalai 2023
G. Kuppan Thirumalai, *A Beginner's Guide to SSD Firmware*,
https://doi.org/10.1007/978-1-4842-9888-6_13

IOPS (input/output operations per second): This refers to the number of read and write operations that the SSD can perform in a given second. This is often used to measure the performance of an SSD under heavy workloads. The higher the IOPS, the better.

Throughput: An SSD's data transfer speed, measured in bytes per second. The higher the throughput, the better, although throughput is affected by elements such as block size and whether the reads and writes are random or sequential.

Latency: Shows how long it takes to process an I/O operation. This process translates to SSD response time and is measured in microseconds or milliseconds. The lower the latency, the better.

Endurance: This refers to the number of write and erase cycles that an SSD can withstand before it begins to experience performance degradation. This metric is mostly used in marketing, like terabytes written (TBW).

Power Consumption: This refers to the amount of power that the SSD consumes while it is in use. This can be important for devices that rely on battery power.

Access Patterns and Test Workloads

An access pattern is the type of storage and retrieval operation going to and from a storage device. Access patterns are described in three main components, as follows:

- Random/Sequential: The random or sequential nature of the data address requests

- Block Size: The data transfer lengths

- Read/Write Ratio: The mix of read and write operations

Any particular workload or test stimulus is approximated by some combination of access patterns. That is, an access pattern is one component of a synthesized equivalent input/output (IO) workload. For example, "RND 4KiB 65:35 R/W" describes an access pattern consisting of a sequence of IO commands, each one 4 KiB long (block size), to random locations on the storage device, in the proportion of 65 percent reads to 35 percent writes.

Workloads

A workload is a set of access patterns observed over a given period of time, such as ten minutes of random 4 KiB 100 percent writes. Key performance metrics, including IOPS, throughput (TP), and latency (LAT), can be described in terms of these access patterns. These metrics can be used to evaluate the performance of a storage device, such as an SSD, under different workloads. Some commonly accepted workloads are random 8KiB 65:35 RW and sequential 128KiB 90:10 RW

Figure 13-1 shows some of the key performance criteria being compared across different SSD manufactures by tech reviewers to help choose an SSD for a specific goal.

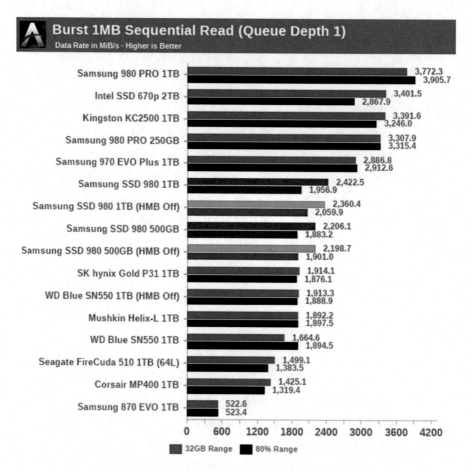

Figure 13-1. *Burst 1 MB sequential read (QD 1)*
Source: Image courtesy [AnandTech] as of Mar-09-2021,
`https://www.anandtech.com/show/16504/the-samsung-ssd-980-5`
`00gb-1tb-review/3`

This figure of sequential read performance uses short bursts of 1 MB, issued as 128 KB operations with no queuing. The burst sequential read performance of the Samsung 980 PRO is marginally faster than its predecessors, but the extra PCIE Gen4 bandwidth does not matter with a queue depth of just one.

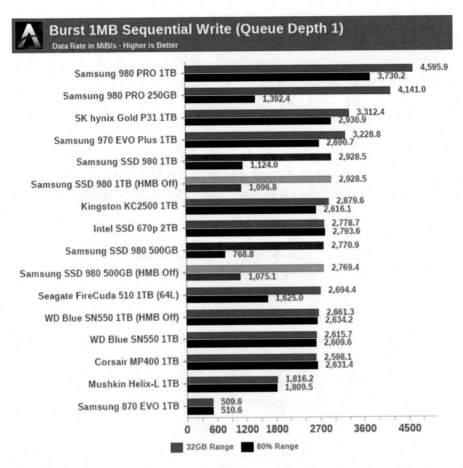

Figure 13-2. *Burst 1 MB sequential write (QD 1)*
Source: Image courtesy [AnandTech]

Typically, the evaluation of sequential write burst performance closely mirrors the procedure used for assessing sequential read burst performance. In this evaluation, each burst entails the writing of 1 MB through 128 KB operations, administered at a queue depth of 1 (QD1). This culminates in the composition of 1 GB of data being written onto a drive housing 16 GB of data.

Historically, the burst sequential write speed metrics for high-end Non-Volatile Memory Express (NVMe) drives have exhibited limited diversity, with a narrow range of scores spanning a wide array of drivers. The advent of PCIe Gen4 drives disrupts this pattern, ushering in tangible enhancements to this QD1 performance aspect. In this test scenario, once again, the victor emerges as the Samsung 980 PRO 1 TB. However, other contenders are making commendable strides, gradually closing the gap.

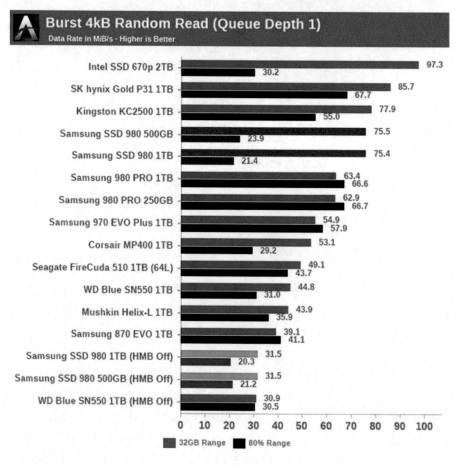

Figure 13-3. Burst 4 KB random read (QD1)
Source: Image courtesy [AnandTech]

The assessment of random read performance entails brief and isolated operations carried out one at a time, without any queuing. To ensure a duty cycle of 20 percent, the drives are provided sufficient idle intervals between bursts, rendering thermal throttling implausible. In each burst, a cumulative total of 32 MB of 4 KB random reads is executed, spanning a 16 GB segment of the disk. The aggregate data read amounts to 1 GB.

While Samsung's 128L TLC, as featured in the 980 PRO, demonstrates improved burst random read latency compared to the earlier TLC iteration, it still lags behind certain competitors; similarly, their 64L MLC, found in the 970 series, follows suit.

In contrast to the 970 EVO Plus, the 980 PRO exhibits modest enhancements in random read performance across the spectrum. However, these differences are marginal. Notably, the PCIe 3 SK hynix Gold P31 capitalizes on similar advantages at higher queue depths and aligns with the QD32 random read throughput of the 980 PRO.

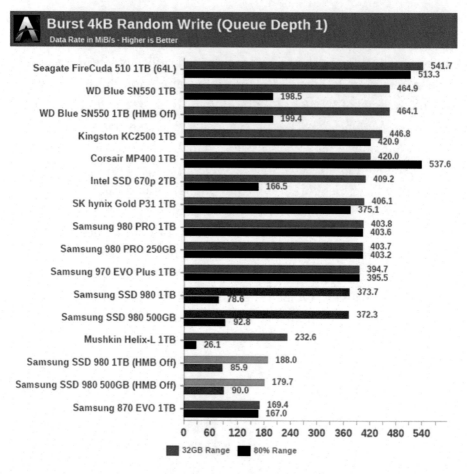

Figure 13-4. *Burst 4 KB random write (QD 1)*
Source: Image courtesy [AnandTech]

The sequential write burst performance test is similar to the sequential read burst performance test. In each burst, 1 MB of data is written as 128 KB operations issued at QD 1. The total test length is 1 GB, and the data is written to a drive containing 16 GB of data.

The burst sequential write speed scores for high-end NVMe drives have been fairly narrow, with a small range of scores for a variety of drives. PCIe Gen4 drives break this trend and deliver real improvements in QD 1 performance. The clear winner in this test is the Samsung 980 PRO 1 TB, but other drives are catching up quickly.

The random write burst performance test is similar to the random read burst test. However, each burst is only 4 MB, and the total test length is 128 MB. The 4 KB random write operations are distributed over a 16 GB span of the drive, and the operations are issued one at a time with no queuing.

The burst random write performance of the Samsung 980 PRO is an improvement over its predecessors. However, Samsung's SLC write cache latency is still significantly slower than that of many of their competitors. PCIe Gen4 support does not seem to be a factor for the 980 PRO at QD 1, and the two capacities of the 980 PRO seem to disagree as to whether the other differences between our old and new testbeds help or hurt. Meanwhile, the Phison-based Seagate FireCuda 510 does seem to benefit significantly from our Gen4 test setup, where it takes a clear lead.

There are several hardware and firmware design factors that can impact the performance of an SSD. Some of these include the following:

Memory Type: Different types of memory, such as NAND flash and 3D XPoint, Hybrid DRAM flash storage, Flash DIMMS, have different performance characteristics.

Memory Architecture: The way in which the memory is organized and accessed can impact performance. For example, using multiple memory channels, having support for multi-plane operations, having die interleave, etc. can increase transfer speeds.

Memory Controller: The memory controller is responsible for managing access to the memory and can impact performance.

Firmware: The firmware on an SSD controls how the device operates and can impact performance. For example, the firmware may implement wear-leveling and garbage-collection algorithms to optimize performance.

Let's look at some more specific strategies that are commonly used in the industry to do well on performance criteria and boost the performance of an SSD through firmware design and implementation, as follows:

Writing to SLC (single-level cell) Blocks Initially: SLC blocks are a type of memory that can store a single bit per cell and are generally faster and more reliable than multi-level cell (MLC) or triple-level cell (TLC) blocks. By writing data to SLC blocks initially, it is possible to improve the performance of the SSD, particularly in terms of write speeds.

Reducing DRAM Access: Many SSDs use DRAM (dynamic random-access memory) as a buffer to store data temporarily before it is written to the NAND flash memory. Accessing the DRAM a lot can make the firmware slower if it is in a critical read or write path, so minimizing the number of times data is transferred between the two can improve performance.

Writing in Parallel: Some SSDs have multiple memory channels, dies (individual memory chips), or planes. By writing data to these different components in parallel, it is possible to improve the overall write speed of the SSD.

Die Interleaving: Die interleaving is a technique in which data is written to multiple dies in a round-robin fashion, rather than writing all the data to a single die. This can improve performance by allowing the SSD to access more dies concurrently, which can increase the effective memory bandwidth. To further increase performance, controllers can take advantage of interleaving. Each NAND flash chip can have multiple dies in it; this is particularly so for high-density parts. 2/4/8 die packs are common. The ability to interleave is dependent on flash/controller/firmware support.

Data Placement: Smart placement of data across the chips of an SSD is critical not only to provide load balancing, but also to affect wear leveling and performance boosting.

Host Interface

NVMe is the fastest interface for SSDs because NVMe uses the PCIe bus instead of the slower SATA interface bus. PCIe 4 can use 32 lanes to transfer data, compared to the four lanes used for SATA SSDs. NVMe SSDs were designed to reduce flash latencies and SSD response time.

Fiber channel is still the highest-performing protocol, but Serial-Attached SCSI (SAS) isn't far behind. Most SSD products built around iSCSI and SATA won't produce 1 million IOPS results unless they have other caching features to assist performance.

These are just a few examples of the strategies that can be used to boost the performance of an SSD through firmware design and implementation. It is important to carefully consider the specific performance requirements of the intended use case and select the appropriate strategies to meet those requirements. Testing and benchmarking the SSD can help to identify areas for improvement and guide the optimization process.

Summary

This chapter has discussed the performance of SSDs. We have seen how the performance of an SSD can be affected by a variety of factors, and how these factors can be optimized through firmware design and implementation. We have also seen how the performance of an SSD can be measured using a variety of benchmarks.

CHAPTER 14

Debugging

In this chapter, we will discuss the debugging of firmware for complex solid-state drives (SSDs). We will start by discussing some of the challenges of debugging firmware, such as the complexity of the firmware code and the difficulty of reproducing the problem. We will then discuss some of the techniques that can be used to debug firmware, such as using a debugger, adding trace output and logging, using simulation or emulation tools, using hardware probes, and using software tools. Finally, we will discuss how to recover a bricked SSD.

Debugging firmware for complex SSDs can be a challenging task, but there are several approaches and techniques that you can use to help identify and resolve issues. Here are some tips and methods that you may find helpful.

Use a debugger. A debugger is a software tool that allows you to execute code one line at a time, set breakpoints, and inspect variables. This can be a very useful tool for understanding how the firmware is executing and identifying where problems may be occurring. To use a debugger, you will need to connect it to the SSD and configure it to work with the firmware. Once the debugger is set up, you can use it to step through the code and inspect variables to understand what is happening at different points in the execution.

Use logging and trace output. Adding trace output and logging to your firmware can provide valuable information about what is happening at different points in the code. This can help you to identify where problems

© Gopi Kuppan Thirumalai 2023
G. Kuppan Thirumalai, *A Beginner's Guide to SSD Firmware*,
https://doi.org/10.1007/978-1-4842-9888-6_14

may be occurring and to understand how the firmware is interacting with other components. To add trace output and logging to your firmware, you will need to add calls to the relevant functions at different points in the code. You can then use a tool to capture the output and view it to understand what is happening.

Use simulation/emulation. In some cases, it may be useful to utilize simulation or emulation tools to test and debug the firmware. These tools allow you to run the firmware in a simulated environment, which can help to identify problems that may not be apparent when running the firmware on hardware. To use simulation or emulation tools, you will need to set up the simulated environment and configure it to work with the firmware. You can then use the tools to run the firmware and analyze the results.

Use hardware probes. Hardware probes, such as JTAG or logic analyzers (NAND, SATA, NVMe), can provide detailed information about the hardware and can be used to trace the execution of the firmware. To use a hardware probe, you will need to connect it to the SSD and configure it to work with the firmware. You can then use the probe to monitor the hardware and trace the execution of the firmware.

Use software tools. There are many software tools available that can help with debugging firmware. For example, there are tools that can analyze memory usage, monitor system performance, and identify potential problems with the firmware without actually testing in hardware. To use these tools, you will need to install them on your development system and configure them to work with the firmware. You can then use the tools to analyze the firmware and identify potential issues like Coverity, Valgrind, etc.

Collect crash dump. Collecting a crash dump when firmware fails or an exception occurs can be a useful way to understand what went wrong and to help identify the cause of the issue. Here are some steps you can follow to collect a crash dump:

- ***Set up crash dump collection.*** Depending on the firmware and the development environment, there may be different ways to set up crash dump collection. Some firmware may have built-in crash dump collection capabilities, while others may require the use of a separate tool. In either case, you will need to set up the crash dump collection feature and configure it to work with your firmware.

- ***Run the firmware.*** Once crash dump collection is set up, you can run the firmware as you normally would. If the firmware fails or an exception occurs, the crash dump collection feature should capture the relevant information and generate a crash dump file that is stored in SSD and retrieved on an as-needed basis.

- ***Collect the crash dump.*** If the firmware fails or an exception occurs, the crash dump collection feature should generate a crash dump file. You can use a tool to access and retrieve the crash dump file from the SSD or other storage location.

- ***Analyze the crash dump.*** Once you have collected the crash dump, you can use a tool to analyze it and understand what went wrong. Depending on the firmware and the development environment, there may be different tools available for analyzing crash dumps. Some common tools include debugger tools and crash dump analysis tools.

Recovering bricked SSD. If an SSD becomes "bricked," it means that it is no longer functioning properly and is unable to boot or perform any operations. There are several potential causes of a bricked SSD, including hardware failures, firmware issues, or problems with the boot process. Here are some steps you can follow to try to recover a bricked SSD:

- ***Check for hardware issues.*** Before attempting to recover a bricked SSD, you should first check for any hardware issues that may be causing the problem. This may involve checking for physical damage to the SSD, verifying that all connections are secure, and running diagnostic tests to check for hardware failures.

- ***Attempt to boot from an alternate boot device.*** In some cases, it may be possible to boot the SSD from an alternate boot device, such as a USB drive or network boot device. This can be helpful if the problem is related to the SSD's boot process or if the SSD's firmware has become corrupted.

- ***Attempt to reflash the firmware.*** If the problem is related to the SSD's firmware, you may be able to recover the SSD by reflashing the firmware. To do this, you will need to connect the SSD to a development system and use a firmware update tool to flash the firmware onto the SSD, or force the firmware into factory mode to update the firmware from factory mode. Reflashing the firmware can be a useful way to recover a bricked SSD if the problem is related to the firmware. Here are some more detailed steps you can follow to reflash the firmware on a bricked SSD:

- ***Prepare the development system.*** To reflash the firmware on a bricked SSD, you will need a development system that is set up to communicate with the SSD. This may involve installing drivers and other software tools, setting up the hardware connections, and configuring the development system to work with the SSD.

- ***Download the firmware.*** You will need to obtain a copy of the firmware that you want to flash onto the SSD. Make sure to download the correct firmware for your SSD and to verify the integrity of the firmware file.

- ***Connect the SSD to the development system.*** Once the development system is prepared, you will need to connect the SSD to the development system. This may involve using a USB or SATA connection, depending on the SSD and the development system.

- ***Put the SSD into boot mode.*** To reflash the firmware, you will need to put the SSD into boot mode. This may involve pressing a specific button or combination of buttons on the SSD, or it may involve issuing a specific command via the development system. Check the manufacturer's documentation for specific instructions on how to put the SSD into boot mode.

- ***Run the firmware update tool.*** Once the SSD is in boot mode and connected to the development system, you can use a firmware update tool to flash the firmware onto the SSD. Follow the instructions provided by the firmware update tool.

- ***Reboot the SSD.*** Once the firmware update is complete, you should reboot the SSD to ensure that the new firmware is properly installed. If the firmware update was successful, the SSD should boot up normally.

- ***Use a hardware probe.*** If the SSD is not responding to normal commands, you may be able to use a hardware probe, such as a JTAG or logic analyzer, to access the SSD at the CPU level. This can be helpful if the problem is related to the SSD's firmware or if the SSD's CPU is not responding to normal commands.

Summary

This chapter has discussed the debugging of firmware for complex SSDs. We have seen the challenges of debugging firmware and the techniques that can be used to do so. We have also seen how to recover a bricked SSD.

CHAPTER 15

Future Developments and Innovations in SSD Firmware

In this chapter, we will discuss the future developments and innovations in solid-state drive (SSD) firmware. As the technology behind SSDs continues to evolve, there are a number of exciting developments and innovations in SSD firmware that are worth exploring. We will start by discussing some of the challenges that SSD firmware developers are facing, such as the increasing complexity of SSDs and the need to support new technologies. We will then discuss some of the promising developments and innovations in SSD firmware, such as host cache mechanisms, QLC support, and expanded hardware support.

On the hardware side, there have been a number of innovations that have contributed to the improved performance and reliability of SSDs. These innovations include the development of new types of NAND flash memory, such as 3D NAND and quad-level cell (QLC) NAND, as well as the use of novel materials and structures, such as conductive bridging random access memory (CBRAM) and phase-change memory (PCM).

On the firmware side, there have been a number of innovations in SSD firmware that have contributed to the improved performance and reliability of SSDs. These innovations include the use of host cache

© Gopi Kuppan Thirumalai 2023
G. Kuppan Thirumalai, *A Beginner's Guide to SSD Firmware*,
https://doi.org/10.1007/978-1-4842-9888-6_15

mechanisms, IO determinism, and streaming concepts, as well as more advanced error correction techniques, such as Reed-Solomon error correction and low-density parity-check (LDPC) codes.

One area of innovation in SSD firmware is the use of host cache mechanisms. These allow the SSD to use the memory of the host system as a cache to improve the performance of read and write operations. This can significantly improve the performance of the SSD, particularly for workloads that involve a high number of small, random read and write operations.

Another area of innovation in SSD firmware is the concept of IO determinism and streaming concepts. IO determinism refers to the ability of the SSD to consistently deliver a predictable level of performance, even under heavy workloads. This is important because it allows users to better understand the performance characteristics of their SSDs and plan their workloads accordingly.

Streaming concepts involve the use of algorithms that optimize the way that data is written to and read from the SSD in order to improve the performance of sequential read and write operations. This is particularly useful for workloads that involve the transfer of large amounts of data, such as video streaming and data backup.

Startup companies are also working on a number of innovative ideas in the field of SSD technology. For example, some startups are focusing on developing new types of memory technology, such as resistive random-access memory (RRAM) and magneto random-access memory (MRAM), which have the potential to improve the performance and reliability of SSDs. Other startups are working on developing new software solutions, such as intelligent data tiering and data deduplication, which can help to improve the efficiency and cost-effectiveness of SSD storage.

Finally, the Flash Memory Summit (https://www.flashmemorysummit.com/), an annual conference that brings together industry experts and researchers in the field of flash memory, is a forum for discussing and sharing innovative ideas in SSD technology. At the Flash Memory Summit, attendees have the opportunity to hear about the latest research and developments in the field, as well as to participate in discussions.

Summary

In summary, there are a number of exciting developments and innovations in SSD firmware that are worth exploring. From host cache mechanisms and QLC support, to expanded hardware support and improved interface protocols, these developments are helping to improve the performance and reliability of SSDs and make them an even more compelling option for storage.

CHAPTER 16

Closing

In this beginner's guide to solid-state drive (SSD) firmware, we have explored the key concepts and techniques that are essential for designing, optimizing, and maintaining SSD firmware. We have looked at the role of firmware in the functioning of SSDs and the importance of keeping the firmware up to date to ensure optimal performance and security. We have also discussed some of the advanced features that are included in modern SSD firmware, such as wear-leveling algorithms, garbage-collection algorithms, error prevention and correction methods, and algorithms to reduce write amplification.

As fellow engineers and professionals, it is important to understand the best practices for designing, optimizing, and maintaining SSD firmware. By understanding the role of firmware in the functioning of SSDs and the various features that are included in modern firmware, we can ensure that our SSDs are performing at their best and are secure against potential threats.

In addition to the concepts and techniques that we have covered in this guide, there are many other tools and resources available to help optimize and maintain SSD firmware. These include hardware probes, such as JTAG and logic analyzers, that can be used to access and troubleshoot SSDs at the CPU level, as well as software tools and utilities that can help us manage and optimize firmware updates and other maintenance tasks.

© Gopi Kuppan Thirumalai 2023
G. Kuppan Thirumalai, *A Beginner's Guide to SSD Firmware*,
https://doi.org/10.1007/978-1-4842-9888-6_16

We hope that this beginner's guide to SSD firmware has been a helpful resource and has provided a basic foundation for understanding the key concepts and techniques that are essential for designing, optimizing, and maintaining SSD firmware. While we have covered basic concepts in this guide, there is much more to learn about every topic. If you are looking to dive deeper into the various aspects of SSD firmware, we recommend keeping an eye out for our next version of this guide, which will go into more detail on each of the topics that we have covered here.

We wish you, the reader, luck in your endeavors to design, optimize, and maintain SSD firmware, and we hope that this guide has been a helpful resource in your journey. Whether you are just starting out in the field of SSD firmware or you are an experienced professional, we hope that you have found something of value in this guide. Thank you for reading, and we hope that you will continue to explore and learn more about this fascinating and important topic.

If you wish to make any comments concerning this book you can do so via gopikt@outlook.com.

My LinkedIn profile: `https://www.linkedin.com/in/gopi-thirumalai/`.

Bibliography

1. LEILEI SONG, KESHAB K. PARHI, ICHIRO KURODA, AND TAKAO NISHITANI. "Hardware/ Software Codesign of Finite Field Datapath for Low-Energy Reed–Solomon Codecs." *IEEE Transactions on Very Large-Scale Integration (VLSI) Systems*, vol. 8, no. 2 (April 2000): 160.

2. JIM COOKE, MICRON TECHNOLOGY, INC. *Flash Memory Technology Direction*. WinHEC, 2007.

3. DAVE HUGHES. "Designing Fail-safe Storage Systems for Embedded Applications." *Embedded Control Europe*, September 2009: 6–7.

4. MICRON TECHNOLOGY, INC. *Wear-leveling Techniques in NAND Flash Devices*. Micron Technology, Inc., October 2008.

5. "Open NAND Flash Interface Specification, Revision 2.2," October 7, 2009, www.onfi.org.

6. MICRON TECHNOLOGY, INC. "NAND Flash Design and Use Considerations," August 2008.

7. THOMAS COUGHLIN. *Digital Storage in Consumer Electronics*. Burlington, MA: Elsevier, Inc., 2008. ISBN-13: 978-0-7506-8465-1

8.   CHRIS RAMSEYER, "Understanding the Different Types of Host Cache," *Tom's Hardware*, June 21, 2018.

9.   CHRIS RAMSEYER, "QLC NAND: The Next Step in Memory and Storage," *Tom's Hardware*, May 23, 2018.

10.   TIM SCHIESSER, "Samsung Announces World's First 4-bit Consumer SSDs," *TechSpot*, March 1, 2018.

11.   BRIAN BEELER, "NVMe: The Next Generation of Solid-State Storage," *StorageReview*, January 8, 2014.

12.   SEAN WEBSTER, "An Introduction to SSD Firmware," *AnandTech*, October 2, 2013.

13.   CHRIS RAMSEYER, "SSD Firmware: The Importance of Keeping It Up to Date," *Tom's Hardware*, September 28, 2013.

14.   https://www.symmetryelectronics.com/blog/
the-development-and-history-of-solid-
state-drives/

15.   https://history-computer.com/ssd-explained-
everything-you-need-to-know/

Index

© Gopi Kuppan Thirumalai 2023
G. Kuppan Thirumalai, *A Beginner's Guide to SSD Firmware*,
https://doi.org/10.1007/978-1-4842-9888-6

Printed in the United States
by Baker & Taylor Publisher Services